Postdevelopmental Approaches to Childhood Research Observation

Postdevelopmental Approaches to Childhood

Series Editors: Jayne Osgood and Mona Sakr

Troubling traditional developmentalist logic, this series brings together postdevelopmental approaches that offer fresh ways to reconsider firmly established ideas about childhood from observations, to policy, curriculum, environment and materials. *Postdevelopmental Approaches to Childhood* gathers a range of international scholars in a series of edited collections that unsettle traditional approaches to practice, pedagogy and research in childhood. Providing a home for innovative, experimental and creative approaches and a diverse range of theoretical and methodological orientations, the series opens up new ways of becoming-with children in both practice and research.

Also Available in the Series:
Postdevelopmental Approaches to Childhood Research Observation,
edited by Jayne Osgood
Postdevelopmental Approaches to Pedagogical Observation in Childhood,
edited by Mona Sakr, Jennifer Rowsell and Kortney Sherbine

Forthcoming in the series:
Postdevelopmental Approaches to Digital Arts in Childhood,
edited by Marissa McClure Sweeny and Mona Sakr
Postdevelopmental Approaches to Play
edited by Jayne Osgood & Victoria de Rijke

Postdevelopmental Approaches to Childhood Research Observation

Edited by
Jayne Osgood

BLOOMSBURY ACADEMIC
LONDON • NEW YORK • OXFORD • NEW DELHI • SYDNEY

BLOOMSBURY ACADEMIC

Bloomsbury Publishing Plc, 50 Bedford Square, London, WC1B 3DP, UK
Bloomsbury Publishing Inc, 1385 Broadway, New York, NY 10018, USA
Bloomsbury Publishing Ireland, 29 Earlsfort Terrace, Dublin 2, D02 AY28, Ireland

BLOOMSBURY, BLOOMSBURY ACADEMIC and the Diana logo are
trademarks of Bloomsbury Publishing Plc

First published in Great Britain 2023
Paperback edition published 2025

Copyright © Jayne Osgood and contributors, 2023

Jayne Osgood and contributors have asserted their right under the Copyright,
Designs and Patents Act, 1988, to be identified as Author of this work.

Series design by Grace Ridge
Cover image © Catherine Falls Commercial / Getty Images

All rights reserved. No part of this publication may be: i) reproduced or
transmitted in any form, electronic or mechanical, including photocopying, recording
or by means of any information storage or retrieval system without prior permission
in writing from the publishers; or ii) used or reproduced in any way for the training,
development or operation of artificial intelligence (AI) technologies, including
generative AI technologies. The rights holders expressly reserve this publication
from the text and data mining exception as per Article 4(3) of the
Digital Single Market Directive (EU) 2019/790.

Bloomsbury Publishing Plc does not have any control over, or responsibility for, any
third-party websites referred to or in this book. All internet addresses given in this
book were correct at the time of going to press. The author and publisher regret
any inconvenience caused if addresses have changed or sites have ceased
to exist, but can accept no responsibility for any such changes.

A catalogue record for this book is available from the British Library.

A catalog record for this book is available from the Library of Congress.

ISBN: HB: 978-1-3503-6973-3
PB: 978-1-3503-6977-1
ePDF: 978-1-3503-6974-0
eBook: 978-1-3503-6975-7

Series: Postdevelopmental Approaches to Childhood

Typeset by Integra Software Services Pvt. Ltd.

For product safety related questions contact productsafety@bloomsbury.com.

To find out more about our authors and books visit www.bloomsbury.com
and sign up for our newsletters.

Contents

List of figures	vi
List of contributors	viii
Series editors' foreword	xiii

Introduction: Postdevelopmental Approaches to Childhood Research Observation *Jayne Osgood* — 1

1. Unflattering Angles: Cameras, Consent and (self) Construction in Visual Classroom Research *Casey Y. Myers* — 11
2. Observing-without-Reading; Material Attractions to Stone and Water *Abigail Hackett and Christina MacRae* — 23
3. Down on the Ground: The Material Memoir of the Posthuman Childhood Researcher *Jayne Osgood* — 39
4. Being there: Observing Care through Doing Nothing in a Toddler Classroom *Teresa K. Aslanian* — 55
5. Telling Story: The Carrier Bag Theory of Fiction as a Means of Reciprocal 'Researching-with' Children *Victoria de Rijke* — 71
6. Humming a Tune: Attending to 'Earworms' as a More-than Observational Practice in Fieldwork with Children *Paulina Semenec* — 95
7. Observing Migrant Children: Shifting from Linguistic Competence to Display of Agency *Federico Farini and Angela Scollan* — 107
8. Toddlers Tinkering with Toys: Following Action Assemblages in Children's Museum Play *Karen Wohlwend, Yanlin Chen, and Adam Maltese* — 127
9. 'Can I Draw in Your Sketchbook?': Collaborative Observation-Making with Children *Hayon Park and Jeffrey Cornwall* — 149

Index — 164

Figures

1.1	Excluded photos of the adult-researcher	16
1.2	Excluded photos of the adult-researcher	17
5.1	Transcript excerpt of class conversation	73
5.2	Poster for exhibition at Cockpit Gallery 1987	73
5.3	L-R drawing the cable release in action	75
5.4	By Yelda. Girls' collages for career choices often included those they would be 'helping' (pupils, animals, etc.) whereas	75
5.5	By Ka is an example of how boys more often depicted themselves as authoritative	75
5.6	*Supertoy* logo designed by children, featuring the hybrid toy 'Captain Bear Beak'	79
5.7	Some 'mutant' toy examples made by children from Headley Primary School, Bristol	80
5.8	Toys made by the public in the Arnolfini gallery	80
5.9	Making in the gallery	80
5.10	*Supertoys* manual	82
5.11	Page of advice to child readers	82
5.12 & 5.13	Children's drawings answering *Who is the boss at home?*	85
5.14	Posters created with children playfully questioning gender/power relations	86
5.15	A page from *Supertoys: A User's Manual* offering synonyms for play; an example of a page directed at both child reader and adult/teacher user, to explore the topic across all play's dynamics	91
6.1	Still from Owen's video	96
6.2	Owen watching his video	102
8.1	Tracking sequence, duration and frequency at exhibit locations	134
8.2	Tracking interactions with materials (instances of hands on toys)	135
8.3	Toddler dropping a ball into the 'Fish Tank' below fish feeding image sign	138

8.4	Attachment pattern: Returning to the nursery to retrieve a baby doll	139
8.5	Reconfiguring doll-crib-child-ground-nurture relations	140
8.6	Firefly nightlight next to crib and wall switch in nursery	142
9.1	Hand puppet drawing	160

Contributors

Dr Teresa K. Aslanian is Associate Professor of Early Childhood Education at the University of South-Eastern Norway (USN). Aslanian holds a PhD in educational science in which she has studied conceptions of care in ECEC and care as a material practice. Her research is included in recent knowledge briefs on the role of kindergarten teachers published by the Ministry of Education and Research. Aslanian has 15 years' experience in ECEC which she draws on to inform her research in Nordic early childhood pedagogy. Her research has resulted in numerous scientific journal publications and book chapters, three edited anthologies, and a book aimed at Norwegian Early Childhood Education teacher students. She is particularly interested in post qualitative inquiry and exploring fundamental concepts in education with various philosophical perspectives.

Dr Yanlin Chen obtained a B.A. in English Language and Literature and a M.A. in Linguistics and Applied Linguistics before taking up an academic post at the University of Science and Technology, Beijing. After pursuing a M.A. in Arts Administration followed a Ph.D. in Curriculum and Instruction at Indiana University Bloomington. Such an interdisciplinary background brought about specializations in multilingual and multimodal literacies, as well as how technologies, materials and space combine to create an inclusive learning environment to encourage children's meaning making in arts organizations like museums.

Dr. Jeffrey M. Cornwall is Assistant Professor of Art Education at Colorado State University. Informed by post-structural thinking and theories of affect, his research focuses on children's learning and making within the public elementary school by engaging critical research and artistic methodologies to think and make with and alongside children. His research has appeared in journals such as *Qualitative Inquiry, Visual Arts Research* and *Studies in Art Education* as well as the book *Visual Arts with Young Children: Practices, Pedagogies, and Learning.*

Dr. Victoria de Rijke is Professor in Arts & Education at Middlesex University in London and Co-Chief Editor of *Children's Literature in Education Journal*. Her research is transdisciplinary across fields of literature and the arts, children's literature, media, play and animal studies, through the associations of metaphor. Her work includes exhibiting arts projects; a picturebook; and numerous academic articles in journals such as: *Contemporary Issues in Early Childhood; Qualitative Inquiry; Education 3–13 International Journal of Primary, Elementary and Secondary years Education; Journal of Literary Education* and *Childhood and Pethood in Literature and Culture*.

Dr Federico Farini is Professor of Sociology at the University of Northampton. He is Visiting Professor at The University of Modena and Reggio Emilia and collaborates with the University of Venice, the European Commission, UNESCO, the Italian Government and the Swiss Government in the support and evaluation of Research. Federico has published nearly 100 scientific works, including books, chapters, articles, in Italian, English, Spanish and Slovenian language. His research activity includes EU-funded research projects concerning inclusive education, intercultural communication, renovation of urban spaces. His current interests concern inequality in access to education and social services, as well as participatory research methods, public sociology and public art projects.

Dr Abi Hackett is a Professor of Childhood and Education at the Institute of Education, Sheffield Hallam University. She is interested in the role of place, materiality and bodies in young children's lives. She researches mostly in community spaces, in collaboration with children and families, employing ethnographic and post-qualitative methods. Abi has recently completed a British Academy Postdoctoral Fellowship to investigate the literacy and language practices of children aged between 12 and 36 months in community spaces. She is currently co-investigator on an inter-disciplinary project titled *Voices of the future: Collaborating with children and young people to re-imagine treescapes*, funded by the Natural Environment Research Council. Her book *More-Than-Human Literacies in Early Childhood*, was published in 2021.

Dr. Christina MacRae is a Research Fellow at Manchester Metropolitan University. She is a former early years teacher, and her research interests lie in early childhood. Her research has a particular focus on sense, affect and movement in children's world-making practices. She has also been involved in research that has focussed on young children's learning in classroom contexts, as well as in museums, galleries and outdoor public space. Christina's most recent research was funded by the Froebel Trust and it used slow-motion video as a method for a co-produced ethnography in a nursery classroom for 2 year-olds.

Dr Adam Maltese is Professor of Teacher Education at Indiana University, Bloomington. His current research involves the collection and analysis of both quantitative and qualitative data regarding student experiences, performance and engagement in science education from elementary school through graduate school.

Dr. Casey Y. Myers is the co-founder of Watershed Community School and a founding member of the Child/Hoods Research Collective, both of which focus on sustainable relationships in the neighborhoods where young children live and learn. Her professional interests include posthumanism, new materialisms, and post-qualitative inquiry in relation to children's every/day lives in school, as well as children's ethical participation in research. Her scholarship has received recognition from international research communities, including the Emerging Scholar Award from the Critical Perspectives on Early Childhood Education SIG of the American Educational Research Association (2020).

Dr. Jayne Osgood is Professor of Childhood Studies at the Centre for Education Research & Scholarship, Middlesex University. Her work addresses issues of social justice through critical engagement with policy, curricular frameworks, and pedagogical approaches. She is committed to extending understandings of 'child' through creative, affective methodologies. She has over 100 publications in the form of books, chapters and journal papers, including *Feminists Researching Gendered Childhoods* (Bloomsbury, 2019) and *Postdevelopmental Approaches to Childhood Art* (Bloomsbury, 2019). She is a long-standing board member at *Contemporary Issues in Early Childhood* and currently journal editor at *Gender & Education* and *Reconceptualising Education Research Methodology*. She is also Book Series Editor for Bloomsbury (*Feminist Thought in Childhood Research* and *Postdevelopmental Approaches to Childhood*) and Springer (*Keythinkers in Education*).

Dr. Hayon Park is an Assistant Professor of Art Education at George Mason University, USA. She is the author of *Rancière and Emancipatory Art Pedagogies: The Politics of Childhood Art* (2023) and co-editor of the anthology *Visual Arts with Young Children: Practices, Pedagogies, and Learning* (2021). She also currently serves as an Associate Director of the Center for the Study of Childhood Art.

Dr Paulina Semenec holds a PhD in Educational Studies from the University of British Columbia (UBC). Her doctoral research explored the various ways that children enact mindfulness in a primary classroom, and she is continuously fascinated by how children's attentional practices (have the possibility to) alter how research can be done. Paulina currently works as an Educational and Evaluation Consultant: Indigenous Initiatives, at the Centre for Teaching, Learning and Technology at UBC. She is honoured to call Squamish – located on the traditional, ancestral and unceded territory of the xʷməθkʷəy̓əm (Musqueam), Squamish and Tsleil-Waututh Nations, her home.

Dr. Angela Scollan is an Associate Professor in Early Childhood Studies at Middlesex University. Angela has over 30 years of practice, research and teaching experience across the discipline of Early Childhood Studies in both FE and HE sectors. Before joining Middlesex University in 2012, for nearly 20 years Angela worked directly with and for children. Her teaching philosophy, research, writing and pedagogical leadership focus on the child first, and the role of a learner within education, as a secondary consideration. She was a researcher on the Erasmus+ *SHARMED* project, and Horizon 2020 *Child Up* project, which worked directly with migrant children and their families to explore the impact of classroom interaction, agency and participation on children's expressions and learning experiences.

Dr Karen Wohlwend is Professor of Literacy, Culture and Language Education at Indiana University, Bloomington. Her research reconceptualizes young children's play as an embodied literacy that produces *action texts* made with moving bodies or animated avatars. Recent work develops nexus analysis methods with a critical sociocultural lens for analyzing the production of shared understanding and belonging, looking closely at the ways children interact with materials and one another as they make sense of their worlds. Her books include *Playing Their Way into Literacies: Reading, Writing, and Belonging in the Early Childhood Classroom; Literacy Playshop: New Literacies, Popular Media, and Playing the Early Childhood Classroom;* and *Literacies that Move and Matter: Nexus Analysis for Contemporary Childhoods.*

Series Editors' Foreword

This book series, *Postdevelopmental Approaches to Childhood*, brings a lively collection of edited volumes together that directly trouble developmentalist logic underpinning dominant ideas about what children can or should (be able to) do at certain stages of development. Although seemingly commonsense and benign, developmentalism is taken up in ways that can lead to the marginalisation of children who do not fit normative expectations, and as a consequence are perceived as deviant, abnormal or substandard (Burman, 2016; Cannella & Viruru, 2004). Through multiple theoretical and practice lenses, postdevelopmentalism offers alternative ways to be with and learn from children and through childhood. It opens up new possibilities for celebrating difference among children and paying closer attention to the unfolding of children's everyday experiences. The series therefore aims to support pedagogues and researchers to experience children and childhood differently, to refuse labels and codification against normative expectations and instead embrace richer perspectives grounded in overt commitments to social justice.

To extend the series, two books focusing on postdevelopmental approaches to observation in childhood are launched simultaneously. The curation of these twin volumes underline how profoundly significant observation is within early childhood. Observation is fundamental to both childhood pedagogies and childhood research and the way observations take shape in contemporary practice builds on long and rich histories, which generates a complex, critical dialogue between developmental and postdevelopmental ways of encountering the world, and the child within the world. This particular volume, edited by Jayne Osgood, focuses on research observations in childhood and what might emerge when such observations are mobilised in ways intended to disrupt developmentalism.

This volume brings together a range of contributions from various geopolitical contexts, and whilst the situatedness of each chapter is significant so too are the threads that weave throughout the entire book. All authors are committed to disrupting developmentalist logic and offering playful accounts of how else research observation can and might take shape. They collectively make evident how approaching observations in experimental and innovative ways can enable the theoretical field of postdevelopmentalism to be extended to develop more open-ended and deeply respectful ways of engaging in observations of/with/for children.

The volume actively ruptures old research orthodoxies, concepts and enactments by calling to account the non-innocence of child observation. Authors insist that childhood studies must move away from the premise that research is either 'on' or 'about' the child. A thread to run throughout the chapters concerns the imperative to research *with* children, as collaborators, co-researchers and inquirers in their own right. Shifting the ways children are constructed through observations creates opportunities for knowledge production to manifest in other ways and for everyone involved in childhood studies to encounter the world differently.

This volume is at pains to stress that postdevelopmental approaches to research observation can never be impartial or objective. Rather researchers must accept themselves as deeply immersed, engaged, and intricately and endless entangled in research contexts. It is by embracing this messy imbrication that the researcher is given the space to slow down, to pause, dwell upon the intensities and uncertainties; and so consider how research seeps into bodyminds, memories and hauntings to tell accounts of childhood that reach beyond individual child subjectivities and measurable performativities.

Postdevelopmental Approaches to Childhood Research Observation then, offers a radical departure from more conventional approaches to childhood studies that are typically in search of evidence, trends and concrete facts on which to intervene when the unpredicted is encountered. For the authors in this volume the lively unpredictability of undertaking research differently gestures towards other ways to conceive of research-with young children that repositions 'child' and the purpose of research. Throughout this volume 'observation' reaches beyond what is witnessed with the eyes, to something that involves all the senses. This book invites researchers to contemplate what might come about when observation goes against the grain to ask what new ways to think about child/hood/s become available when research is radically rethought and practiced differently.

Introduction: Postdevelopmental approaches to childhood research observation

Jayne Osgood
Middlesex University, UK

This volume makes an important contribution to the series *Postdevelopmental Approaches to Childhood*. Postdevelopmentalism is a growing, critical force in childhood studies and offers a timely antidote to a long-standing preoccupation with linear child development and the predominant idea that children can be understood against normative ages and stages, which is often assessed through objective research observation. This volume dismantles such ideas by offering lively accounts of how research observation, framed by postdevelopmental approaches, in childhood studies can take on myriad dimensions that pursue an altogether different logic. This book invites readers to be open to surprises and to engage in delightfully difficult questions about childhood, the reasons research with children so often involves adult-directed observation, and what else can come into view when ideas about children, research and observation are reconfigured.

Moving beyond developmentalism in childhood research observation

This book challenges dominant developmental models of observation in early childhood research. It deconstructs traditional approaches to observation, which tend to focus on 'capturing' development in action. It explores alternative ways of thinking about and doing observations in early childhood, particularly observations typically undertaken by adults as part of research investigations.

The contributors are inspired by a diverse range of theoretical perspectives that challenge traditional developmentalist approaches, including posthumanism, feminist new materialism, social semiotics and sociocultural approaches.

Observations are frequently a cornerstone to early childhood research projects. Observation is a dominant mode of inquiry used in the pursuit of finding ways to know (and fix) the developing child against normative expectations. Childhood scholars are taught how to go in search of certain forms of knowledge about children and childhood that can be discovered through careful, directed and prescribed observational techniques. Typically, how we think about and conduct observations is deeply connected with dominant developmental paradigms in early childhood, where the observation tracks the processes through which the child is moving towards adulthood and full competence. Troubling developmentalism and its capacity to both marginalize children that do not fit 'normal' patterns of development (Burman, 2008) and miss the richness of childhood experiences (Sakr & Osgood, 2019) therefore means also troubling our approach to observations in early childhood. The prevailing approaches to observation in childhood studies are limiting and present social justice dilemmas that must be unsettled, dismantled and reimagined. Approaching observations in new, experimental and innovative ways can enable the theoretical field of postdevelopmentalism to be extended and develop new, more open-ended and deeply respectful ways of engaging in observations of/with/for children.

How postdevelopmentalism takes shape in this book

Researching-with

Collectively the chapters in this book work to actively rupture old research orthodoxies, concepts and enactments. In various ways, the non-innocence of child observation is called to account and an insistence that childhood studies must move away from the premise that research is either 'on' or 'about' the child. There is a traceable thread running throughout the chapters concerning the imperative to research *with* children, that is, engaging with children as collaborators, co-researchers and inquirers in their own right. Shifting the ways in which children are framed through research observations generates important and exciting ways to engage with both knowledge production and our relationship to the world around us.

'Learning again' as childhood researchers

As contributors to this volume make clear, such a shift in how we understand and engage with children throughout research encounters demands that adults, in this case researchers, radically reappraise themselves. Researching at a distance in the name of objectivity is almost impossible in encounters with very young children since their curiosity and bodily interruptions are omnipresent and determine the conditions of possibility. At-a-distance research is not only challenging to undertake, but it also misses multiple layers of rich insights and provocations with which childhood scholars can wrestle and theorize to reach other accounts of childhood. Throughout this volume, the resistance to the 'god trick' (identified by Haraway (1988) and taken up by early childhood scholars, e.g. Osgood, 2019) underlines an imperative for researchers to recognize how deeply enmeshed they are in that which they research. As we see throughout chapters in this book, getting down on the ground; sharing notebooks, sketchbooks, recording devices; crafting together; tinkering with toys, and generally allowing ourselves to be deeply affected by what we see, hear and sense in early childhood contexts pushes research in novel directions. Postdevelopmental approaches turn observation back onto the observer by demanding that what it is to research, to be a researcher, is called to account. When researchers are caught out of time and out of place, rather than rushing to intervene to correct the unplanned directions that research is heading, we might instead pause, dwell upon the intensities and uncertainties; and contemplate the various ways that research seeps into bodyminds, memories and hauntings to tell rich and confederate accounts of childhood that reach beyond individual child subjectivities.

This volume attests to the significant learning that becomes part of postdevelopmental childhood studies for everyone involved. A willingness for researchers to unlearn, to set aside notions of mastery and expertise aligned with established research orthodoxies about the 'right way' to undertake observation can agitate ways to 'learn again' (Haraway, 2016). It is important that researchers grapple with the difficult questions that arise from undertaking observation differently, specifically about the implications of human exceptionalism, and an adult-centric exceptionalism at that. Shifting how, when and where research observation happens is important ethic-onto-epistemological work. Allowing the researcherly self to be disturbed by the seemingly mundane and unremarkable creates a means of accessing the unknown and unknowable. This speculative knowing is a radical departure from more conventional approaches to childhood studies that are typically in search of evidence, trends and concrete facts on which to intervene when the unpredicted is encountered. For the authors in this volume, it is precisely the unpredictable that provides the focus of their inquiries and so gestures towards other ways to research-with young children.

Troubling the I/eye of childhood observation

A visual optics has long been the preferred means of capturing some form of representation of reality as it unfolds in childhood contexts. This book unsettles the privileging of the all-seeing I/eye of the childhood researcher. Instead, questions are posed about images, photographs and visual accounts that are not in pursuit of representation or an account of facts gathered about child development. 'Observation' reaches beyond what is witnessed with the eyes, rather it involves all the senses, and not only the researcher's either. Multi-sensory observations attend to the ways in which the young child becomes-with, through encounters, entanglements and interactions with space, matter, sounds, textures, movements and atmospheres. A thread running through several chapters is the atmospheric: attunement to atmospheres, the impression that sonic atmospheres leave and paying attention to atmospheres that are rarely registered. Invisible forces that resist human explanation cannot be captured by visual optics. This book invites researchers to contemplate what might come about when observation goes against the grain; when hauntings that are agitated are taken seriously and pursued tentacularly. What new ways become available to think about child/hood/s differently?

Slowing down: Another science is possible

The invitation to slow down, to step aside, but simultaneously deeply immerse in research encounters – is implicit within all the contributions to this volume. What might happen if researchers literally 'did nothing'? What does resisting the urge to fall into methodological orthodoxies make possible? When we allow research to seep into pores and sinews what new stories about childhood are given opportunities to surface? This slow scholarship (Stengers, 2015) is not about capturing neat, readily recognizable data or some coherent account of child/hood/s. When the objective becomes to wallow, to allow ourselves to attune to atmospheres and relationalities so that affects are sensed, registered and permitted to linger on, the frame of our inquiries becomes simultaneously more intricate, complex and infinitely more confederate. Research and accounts of research become unfamiliar and unsettling, in part because they are disposed to directly address concerns about our human condition and worldly connection which can be explored through seemingly insignificant moments and happenings that would otherwise be overlooked.

The chapters in this book

The volume opens with a chapter from Casey Myers who offers an insightful, playful and candid exploration of what happens to researchers through research-with children. She pays attention to the ways in which adults might become different through the observational modalities of childhood research. By working with photographic data generated with young children over the course of a year, Myers pays renewed attention to herself as the adult researcher. A series of photos that she has unwittingly, and perhaps unwillingly, been involved in generating are revisited to raise important questions about what counts as data, consent and the messy realities of researching-with children. As a researcher frequently working with cameras in the classroom, Myers finds herself the owner of countless photos of *herself* that were not consented to. By deploying a post-qualitative and new materialist approach Myers explores the ways in which camera+children+researcher produce novel relational events rather than capturing and representing static moments in time.

In the second chapter, Abigail Hackett and Christina MacRae attempt to 'see without reading', which is a practice of finding ways to connect with experiences of young children without reading them according to dominant meaning systems. They resist making sense of the child and instead sense matter as ways to foreground more-than-human dimensions of events that animate them as researchers rather than explaining child behaviour. They explore ways to witness what is sensed through atmospheres and alternative timescales and relationalities. Two specific events from research provide the focus: a child's play in a puddle outside a nursery and an encounter between a child and a piece of ironstone in a museum. Hackett and MacRae explore how images, held in the mind's-eye, unsettle the strangle-hold of observation as a practice of close noticing and swift reading for meaning. They go on to consider how these accumulating felt events of children/puddles/stones can assist in foregrounding geo-political histories of matter that can be activated as they hover in the atmosphere. Their ultimate goal in undertaking this mode of research is to resist making sense of the child, and instead by sensing matter, identify invisible forces that resist human explanation but animate children's common worlds. ·

Next, Jayne Osgood wonders where (else) the residues of observation might take childhood inquiries. She proposes taking a confederate and speculative approach to 'observation' that traces the bodily immersion of the researcher within broader power structures that underline the material affects of 'what counts' when research is reconfigured. She stresses that observation in childhood research is typically associated with what can be seen and registered and so privileges a visual optics – of what can be immediately witnessed with the eyes (or camera lens). Consequently, researchers have become accustomed to making sense of what is seen; what observations can tell us about the child, in the moment, against some narrow imaginary. Osgood wonders what might happen to observation in early childhood contexts when other optics are elevated – that allow observation to become sensed, haptic, bodily encounters whereby memories and hauntings of life in the Anthropocene are agitated. By working with the concept of transcorporeality this chapter asserts that human bodies (both the young child and adult researcher) are porous and materially discursively altered by the landscapes in which they are shaped, and in turn shape. The 'material memoir' provides a means to trace transcorporeality and so rupture ordinary knowledge practices by observing the material, entangled reality of 'self'. Such memoirs involve negotiating hazardous landscapes of risk and toxicity in order to disrupt and enlarge ideas about what (else) 'observation' might become and make possible.

In Chapter 4, Teresa K. Aslanian explores the limitations of recording, sight and seeing, and the potentially generative process of doing nothing during observations. She explores what happened when the search for an observable example of care beyond the human dyad in an early childhood classroom for toddlers could not be found. Finding her research temporarily derailed, she put down pen, paper and iPhone, and decided to do nothing. She theorizes the richness and generative possibilities of 'doing nothing' as 'being there'. A slow and deep immersion in the not-known leads her to explore the entanglement of humans and equipment and question the idea of seeing as a unidirectional act. Bringing a range of philosophies together, Aslanian explores how observation as a process of 'being there' might be approached as a postdevelopmental strategy to resist methodological orthodoxies and a means to generate different knowledge, about the seemingly unremarkable, differently.

In Chapter 5, Victoria de Rijke offers something of a (collective) biographical account of 'researching-with' children. With the help of Le Guin's *Carrier Bag Theory of Fiction* de Rijke presents a long and lively story of collaborative, inclusive approaches to childhood research observation where children are taken seriously, as co-researchers. The chapter questions the notion of the recipient in research involving children: the (unseen/unknown) grant awarded, the (adult/academic) audience and reception, largely ignoring the 'researched-upon' child. She contends that when children are 'researched-with' reciprocally, they become the key recipients of observations and findings. She moves backward and forward in time as a reciprocal method arguing for postdevelopmental, agential observations in practice research, looking closely and critically at her experiences of working collaboratively and persistently challenging the need for determinacy or closure – as either creative output or research evidence.

Paulina Semenec attends to 'earworms' as a more-than observational practice in fieldwork with children. In her chapter, Semenec responds to the haunting sonic atmosphere of an early childhood classroom that became registered as 'data'. She attends to, and takes seriously, a child humming a popular song that dominated the space during her fieldwork in a grade three classroom. The song became an 'earworm' that occupied her thoughts during fieldwork, and long afterwards. The child humming had been identified as having a special educational need, and was frequently deemed unable to pay attention, sit still or focus. Semenec examines how tuning into the vibrational affect produced by the earworm held the potential to disrupt developmentalist discourses that frame this child in narrow and deficit terms. Attending to the repetition and incoherence of the earworm generated alternative readings of a particular child humming/singing in a self-recorded video, one that disrupts linear narratives that claim to know him. Rather than focus solely on observations of individual children's behaviours and intentions, attending to sound/earworms can make room for the complexities of childhood and so open more creative and equitable relations between children and researchers.

In Chapter 6, Federico Farini and Angela Scollan challenge the prevailing discourse about the importance of language competence for migrant children through their observation of observations in multilingual settings. Their analysis of video-recorded interactions involving children and teachers at an Italian *Scuola dell'infanzia*, influenced by the Reggio Emilia Approach, was committed to positioning all children as competent agents. This approach allowed a shift in the frame of teachers' observation, from *linguistic competence* to *participation in communication*, and a shift in expectations from migrant children as deficient to a recognition and promotion of their agency. The chapter focuses on two interrelated aspects of the video-recorded interactions to argue that teachers' and children's ideas and practices regarding talk may promote shared personal expressions of ideas, emotions and experiences, accessing the agentic status of authors of knowledge.

Next, Karen Wohlwend, Yanlin Chen and Adam Maltese look beyond developmentalist assumptions about very young children; specifically, that their engagements with educational technology is only ever individual, imitative and partial. The authors use sociomaterial theory to shift the focus from individual behaviours to actions co-produced in child-toy-text assemblages, by attending to the intra-actions among children and toys as well as the play histories embedded in toys and the physical space. Video data is examined to unearth assemblage actions as embodied readings of materials and spaces expressed through explorations with toys. Children's embodied readings of toys conflicted with designers' assumptions that the museum exhibit materials would evoke orderly problem-solving and vocabulary development. Toddlers' tinkering though revealed that action assemblages were fluid, repetitive and temporary configurations of moving bodies and toys, rather than driven by intentionality. Toys and materials acted as catalysts conveying powerful messages to toddlers leading to immediate, often non-verbal responses. When research lenses are expanded to acknowledge the contribution of the material environment as well as embodied playful and exploratory pretence that leaves no trace, important possibilities are generated to conceptualize the child in observation differently.

Finally, the volume concludes with a chapter from Hayon Park and Jeffrey Cornwall that considers how research might be created *with* children through a concept and practice of 'observation-making'. The authors define observation-making as a deeply subjective, relational collaboration that emerges as adult researcher and children open to being affected by and affecting each other. By challenging dominant, hierarchical modes of childhood research and observation, where the adult seeks to observe children to capture knowledge *about* children, the authors explore observation as a relational concept and practice that is created with them. As art education researchers, Park and Cornwall participated in individual research in early childhood spaces in the United States, both experienced a common phenomenon of the notebook intended for ethnographic fieldnotes becoming a *sketchbook,* where collaborative drawing between the adult researcher and children emerged. The chapter discusses the instrumentality of the researcher notebook in relation to thinking about the sketchbook as a body with the capacity to affect and be affected, insisting that research and making observations with children should be reimagined.

In summary, this volume illustrates the possibilities that exist for research observation in childhood contexts to be radically rethought and practised differently. This collection urges that postdevelopmental approaches to childhood observation might best be thought of as a playful archive of affect rather than a coherent, accumulating body of knowledge. It involves a shift in gaze from reading child/hood/s in terms of what a child can do, and what an observation means, to attending to the matter that matters in research, and the relationalities that form within minor moments and encounters.

This book provides glimpses into alternative approaches that are taken to researching-with children that privilege a mode of coming to 'know' children through inventive, creative, subversive, sensorial, experimentation. With this orientation, research observation exceeds what is observed in the conventional sense, and urges childhood scholars to take seriously the 'what else' that surfaces and agitates us in the moment. Research observation becomes a much more expansive and intensive process that demands researchers attune to what is sensed, heard, smelt, ingested, registered, and that which resurfaces and haunts months or maybe years after. By approaching childhood studies in this way, we are called upon to persistently question what it is, that really matters in childhood research observation.

References

Burman, E. (2008). *Developments: Child, Image, Nation.* London: Routledge.
Haraway, D. J. (1988). Situated knowledges: The science question in feminism and the privilege of the partial perspective. *Feminist Studies 14*(3), 575–99.
Haraway, D. J. (2016). *Staying with the Trouble: Making Kin in the Chthulucene.* Durham: Duke University Press.
Osgood, J. (2020). Becoming a 'mutated modest witness' in early childhood research. In C. Shulte (Ed.), *Ethics and Research with Young Children: New Perspectives* (pp. 113–27). London: Bloomsbury.
Sakr, M. & Osgood, J. (Eds.) (2019). *Postdevelopmental Approaches to Childhood Art.* London: Bloomsbury.
Stengers, I. (2015). *Another Science Is Possible: A Manifesto for Slow Science.* London: Polity.

Unflattering angles: Cameras, consent and (self) construction in visual classroom research

Casey Y. Myers

Watershed Community School, Kent, OH USA

Introduction

Over the past thirty years, major shifts within the field of qualitative research have led to disruptions in the conceptualization and actualization of visual methods generally, and in the role of photographic images in particular – moving away from the sole use of photographs created and/or collected by researchers *about* research participants and towards the inclusion of image data generated by those engaged within collaborative, participatory inquiry (Pink, 2013). The popularity of participatory research, as well as the increased consideration of children's rights frameworks, has afforded qualitative research within childhood studies and early childhood education to mirror these larger trends; whereas formerly photographic images might only be produced by the adult researcher in order to create visual representations of children, their activities, and/or their artefacts for the purposes of recording and analysing childhood phenomena, photography is currently widely considered an accessible and equitable way for *children* to capture and represent their own perspectives (e.g. Clark & Moss, 2001, 2005; Clark, 2008).

Regardless of these shifts in methods around participation and visual data generation, the vast majority of visual methodologies conceptualize the camera as a documentary tool and the photograph as a representational artefact. Marked by 'methodological instrumentality' these methods, despite their recognition of the utility of more collaborative modes of data production between researcher and participant, continue to exist 'within the humanist enclosure, grounded in humanist concepts of language, reality, knowledge, power, truth, resistance, and the subject' (Lather, 2013, p. 635). These approaches continue to operate on a Cartesian premise – that images are a means to disentangle phenomena (Hultman & Lenz Taguchi, 2010). Within the past decade, however, a growing interest in *post-qualitative inquiry* (St. Pierre, 2011; Lather & St. Pierre, 2013) has made room for conceptualizing image-data as emerging through intricate and dependent sets of material-discursive circumstances, and this has had consequences for the ways in which the generation, analysis and reporting of visual data is enacted across fields of study. Post-qualitative inquiry involves making moves towards questioning, disrupting or displacing 'humanist optics' – what Lather (2013) calls the 'settled places in our work' (p. 632). This has often resulted in researchers taking up diffractive analyses to push against humanist conceptions and enactments of reflection, reflexivity and representation (e.g. Mazzei, 2013, 2014; MacLure, 2013; Lenz Taguchi, 2013). Abandoning allegiance to the *all-seeing eye/all-knowing I* forces us to deterritorialize habits around the idea of photographic images as 'observational' records, as static, representational artefacts that allow us to accurately capture and review past events. Within a post-qualitative landscape, the generation of and engagement with photographic images within research is conceptualized as the on-going production of constructed, agential cuts of events (Barad, 2003). There is no clear point wherein a photo begins and ends, as these image-data-events continue to be impacted by and productive of the entangled relations of the time-space-mattering of inquiry (Lenz Taguchi, 2010, 2013).

Although post-qualitative inquiry within the field of early childhood can be considered an emerging or minor movement, there have been several who have taken-up this post-qualitative orientation towards visual methodologies with young children, conceptualizing and enacting photography and photo data as sites of productive entanglement (e.g. Anggård, 2015; Kind, 2013; Murphy, 2020; Myers, 2017, 2019). It is with/in this particular set of onto-epistemological and methodological commitments that this chapter emerges. Specifically, this work engages with a series of images I have unwittingly (unwillingly?) taken part in generating during a long term, post-qualitative classroom inquiry with young children and asks what these images might continue to produce, long after the research has 'officially' concluded. As a researcher who brings cameras into the early years classroom, I have come to be in possession of many, many photos of *myself* to which I did not specifically consent and/or do not actually remember the children taking. These images were never discussed or attended to by the children with whom I researched. These photos were not selected, neither by me nor by the children, for inclusion in any of the prior publications associated with this research project. By placing these heretofore excluded, overlooked or unwanted images of myself within the larger context of a post-qualitative classroom inquiry with children and cameras, my aim is to grapple with the ways in which the researching 'self' might emerge when images are understood as agential, constructed cuts of the time-space-mattering of research. Utilizing a post-qualitative and new materialist orientation to explore the ways in which camera+children+researcher produce novel relational events (rather than neatly capture and represent static moments in time), I aim to interrogate conceptions the self, reckoning with 'unflattering angles' in both the literal and figurative sense.

In the sections that follow, I lay out a brief overview of the ways in which the production of images emerged within a year-long post-qualitative classroom inquiry with young children. A description of these improvised, messy assemblages of methods are placed alongside these 'self' images as diffractive encounter, a method of attending to the 'interactive re-configuring of patterns of differentiating/entangling' (Barad, 2014, p. 168). That is, the goal of analysis here is not to glean the deeper meanings of these photos in terms of what they represent, but to highlight the ways in which encountering these novel assemblages of photographic data produce *differences* and that these are, perhaps, 'differences that make a difference' (Barad, p. 49 in Dolphijn & van der Tuin, 2012) in conceptions and enactments of adult-researcher. In this way, the images that children constructed of me serve as both the content *and* the method for this chapter. This is my attempt to locate myself within the so-called observational tools of research when the idea(l)s around both concepts and enactments of images are ruptured. The chapter concludes with my thoughts about what these images continue to *do*, and how the 'researching self' emerges, solidifies or comes undone when photographs are understood to be productive events rather observational tools.

Diffracting (self) data

From 2013 to 2014, I spent a year mapping the meaning-matter relations that comprised classroom events in collaboration with sixteen kindergarten children. We spent a good deal of time reworking and renegotiating methods of more traditional participatory inquiry, such as participant observation, interviews and photo documentation. The result was a messy, improvised method assemblage rather than a systematized, linear progression of methods wherein each step is cleanly divided from the next (Law, 2004). Not only were the methods themselves contingent upon each other, but they were also constantly being disrupted by the assemblages already at work in the research context that were also shifting from moment to moment. Within these flexible boundaries, the goal of inquiry shifted from 'knowing' social realities by systematically separating their components to 'relating' to multiple material-discursive realities by being part of the machines that produce them. We played and composed photos, drawings and narratives in a constantly shifting collaboration, not as objective or representational records, but rather as 'constructed cuts' of the ongoing intra-actions between children and myself and other 'things'. The children would come to call these methods 'being with', 'doing photos' and 'becoming cameras'

Being with

The more traditional role of participant observation was subverted in favour of engaging in the flow of people and materials at play in the classroom. When the conception of 'participant observer' was actualized as 'being with', there was no clear division between building rapport and familiarity with children and witnessing and photographically documenting 'naturally' occurring events. According to the children, an appropriate way of 'being with' them was not to sit to the side observing, but to more actively engage in whatever events were occurring. I was mindful to take cues from the children (e.g. obtaining permission to 'be with' or waiting to be asked, asking permission to photograph and allowing them to use my camera to compose their own photos, noticing and acting on behalf of play schemes already in motion, etc.). Once I 'be(came) with' them the flow of events and relationalities were always altered, so the boundary between our subjectivities and the field of relations was constantly in flux. In these assemblages, we produced something different than we could have if we were not becoming together.

Doing photos

Instead of interviewing children about what the images we had co-constructed in the classroom meant or represented, we would intra-act with these images noticing what they would 'do' to us and with us – inciting us to tell stories, to draw or write, or to construct new images in response. The children came to call this active entanglement with and reworking of classroom photo documentation 'doing photos'. We spent months engaging daily in 'doing photos' sessions; the children decided when and with which classmates these sessions would occur, and what photos, narratives and drawings we would explore.

Becoming cameras

Several months into our inquiry, I introduced a set of cameras to the classroom, explaining to children how they could be used to take photos of whatever they deemed was important. All the children in the class had access to the cameras for several months. Some children used the cameras frequently, others only sporadically, as there were no requirements for using the cameras other than a desire to do so. The children experimented with how 'child + camera = becoming camera' was a powerful machine, able to enter into and incite new events that altered classroom relations. After introducing these cameras, the children would move freely between 'my' photos and 'theirs' during our 'doing photos' sessions depending on our conversations and the ways in which our photo-doings unfolded. Within the classroom, the children tended to use the cameras to incite new becomings, such as stopping the action, entering another child's play space, transgressing the limits placed by another child or otherwise working the boundaries of bodies and discourses as cameras were put to work. Children's becoming (with) cameras produced new sites of material discursivity that were not always about constructing a particular image, but were more about making something happen (Kind, 2013). The camera's presence as a material agent was entangled with children in producing new events; many events of importance to the children were not captured with the camera but were produced (in part) by it.

Constructing the *Kindergarten Book*

In the generation of these layers and layers of data events, children were aware of my intention to construct a dissertation, something they called *The Kindergarten Book* (Myers, 2019). We had many discussions around whether to use pseudonyms (what they called 'privacy names') or not and how they could determine the re-presentation of our work together. The children and I engaged in an ongoing process of generation and revision, as they determined which events should be re-told and how, which photos and drawings should be

Figure 1.1 Excluded photos of the adult-researcher.

Figure 1.2 Excluded photos of the adult-researcher.

applied to those re-presentations, and I refined the narratives and connected them to various scholarly or popular literatures in my writing. They could also permanently 'delete' any photos, drawings, videos, audio recordings that we made so that they would not be included in the book. They often invoked this right. Other photographs, drawings and narratives, were simply put aside and were not discussed at all, let alone chosen for inclusion in the *Kindergarten Book*.

Humanist hauntology of images

What kinds of onto-epistemological, ethical, methodological and axiological complexities come into play in this diffractive space – the productive entanglement between visual methodologies with children and these heretofore discarded images of the adult-researcher? And what is left unsettled? These image-data have become 'hauntings and troublings that exert a pull and that won't let go of the past, as if it is in the past' (Mazzei, 2016, p. 159). And placing my methodological commitments in relation to these 'self' images has allowed me to 'feel my way into a different analytic space that was not particularly comfortable' (Lather, 2016, p. 126). What this work brings to the fore, for me, are the ways in which humanism has continued to operate on me, on my conception of images, on observing and being observed.

Despite claiming a relational, radical onto-epistemology in my research with children and (still) conceptualizing images as sites of on-going material-discursive production and data as a constitutive force, I realize now that I had settled on the assumption that these particular photos of myself somehow didn't *matter*, either figuratively or literally. That is, I carried on as if these images were not *important* to the research because they were not discussed or selected by the children for inclusion in publications or other re-presentations of our inquiry. And I also stopped considering how they might be working, what they might be capable of doing once the inquiry was 'complete'. In doing so, I realize I relegated these discarded images to the kind of passive, humanist optics that I thought I had made a commitment to undoing.

In my inquiries with children, I make a commitment to research as an *intervention* into the world (Barad, 1999; Hultman & Lenz Taguchi, 2010). This entails recognizing the ways in which researcher and participants and data never pre-exist each other, as all emerge as phenomena-in-relation. I can recognize now that I have been less willing to acknowledge the ways in which these particular image-data, these constructed cuts of material discursive relations, are capable of intervening on me and my own researcher subjectivities. By disregarding these images, I was able to construct myself as an adult-researcher willing to listen, to take seriously the choices of the children with whom I researched. I never probed for details as to why these particular photos were taken or why they were not included. I was able to frame why I did or didn't do these things as a matter of ethics, foregrounding the participatory power of the children with whom I researched. But was I *too* willing to disregard images of myself? Diffractively working these image-data in the present, I can't separate my willingness to set these images aside from the affects they produce. How I *feel* in the moments when I 'see' them, the sensations and resignations that stir in my researcher-self as I contend with gaze, upon gaze, upon gaze – these indeed must matter, too. My thick legs and fat arms, my unposed face, my uncertain expression, the 'observed' and 'constructed' (and much younger) body of a researcher doing research, are all bound-up in my so-called ethical choices. Engaging diffractively with these images now produces a renewed awareness that my post-qualitative ethics needs to keep evolving in order to continually 'contest and rework what matters and what is excluded from mattering' (Barad, 2007, p. 178),

According to Mazzei (2013), within the landscape of post-qualitative inquiry there is no 'division between a field of reality (what we ask, what our participants tell us, and the places we inhabit), a field of representation (research narratives constructed after the interview), and a field of subjectivity (participants and researchers)' (p. 735). Indeed, in the years since the 'completion' of this research project, these image-data events continue to work on me; the boundaries between what is *done* with images and what images *do* become increasingly blurred.

My aim in producing this chapter is not to provide any concrete answers or practical solutions for a 'better' visual research practice or a more nuanced interpretation of images. Instead, I simply propose an increased fluidity, not only in the ways in which researchers conceptualize and engage with visual data events, but also in what 'counts' as meaningful constructions of the researching 'self' and when these knowings-doings might occur within the time-space-mattering trajectory of research.

References

Anggård, E. (2015). Digital cameras: Agents in research with children. *Children's Geographies, 13*(1), 1–13.

Barad, K. (1999). Agential realism: Feminist interventions in understanding scientific practices. In M. Biagioli (Ed.), *The Science Studies Reader* (pp. 1–11). New York: Routledge.

Barad, K. (2003). Posthumanist performativity: Towards an understanding of how matter comes to matter. *Signs, 28*(3), 801–31.

Barad, K. (2007). *Meeting the Universe Halfway: Quantum Physics and the Entanglement of Matter and Meaning*. Durham, NC: Duke University Press.

Barad, K. (2014). Diffracting diffraction: A cutting together-apart. *Parallax, 20*, 168–87.

Clark, A. (2008). Ways of seeing: Using the mosaic approach to listen to young children's perspectives. In A. Clark, A. T. Kjørholt, & P. Moss (Eds.), *Beyond Listening: Children's Perspectives on Early Childhood Services* (pp. 29–50). Portland, OR: The Policy Press.

Clark, A. & Moss, P. (2001). *Listening to Young Children: The Mosaic Approach*. London: National Children's Bureau.

Clark, A. & Moss, P. (2005). *Spaces to Play: More Listening to Young Children using the Mosaic Approach*. London: National Children's Bureau.

Dolphijn, R. & van der Tuin, I. (2012). *New Materialism: Interviews and Cartographies*. London: Open Humanities Press.

Hultman, K. & Lenz Taguchi, H. (2010). Challenging anthropocentric analysis of visual data: A relational materialist methodological approach to educational research. *International Journal of Qualitative Studies in Education, 23*(5), 525–42.

Jackson, A. Y. (2013). Posthuman data analysis of mangling practices. *International Journal of Qualitative Studies in Education, 26*(6), 741–8.

Kind, S. (2013). Lively entanglements: The doings, movements and enactments of photography. *Global Studies of Childhood, 3*(4), 427–41.

Lather, P. (2013). Methodology-21: What do we do in the afterward? *International Journal of Qualitative Studies in Education, 26*(6), 634–45.

Lather, P. (2016). Top ten+ list: (Re)Thinking ontology in (post)qualitative research. *Cultural Studies ↔ Critical Methodologies, 16*(2), 125–31.

Lather, P. & St. Pierre, E. A. (2013). Post qualitative research. *International Journal of Qualitative Studies in Education, 26*(6), 629–33.

Law, J. (2004). *After Method: Mess in Social Science Research*. New York: Routledge.

Lenz Taguchi, H. (2010). *Going beyond the Theory/Practice Divide in Early Childhood Education: Introducing An Intra-active Pedagogy*. New York: Routledge.

Lenz Taguchi, H. (2013). Images of thinking in feminist materialisms: Ontological divergences and the production of researcher subjectivities. *International Journal of Qualitative Studies in Education, 26*(6), 706–16.

MacLure, M. (2013). Researching without representation? Language and materiality in post-qualitative methodology. *International Journal of Qualitative Studies in Education, 26*(6), 658–67.

Mazzei, L. (2013). A voice without organs: interviewing in posthumanist research. *International Journal of Qualitative Studies in Education, 26*(6), 732–40.

Mazzei, L. A. (2014). Beyond an easy sense: A diffractive analysis. *Qualitative Inquiry, 20*(6), 742–6.

Mazzei, L. (2016). Voice without a subject. *Cultural Studies ↔ Critical Methodologies*, *16*(2), 151–61.

Molloy Murphy, A. (2020). *Animal Magic, Secret Spells, and Green Power: More-Than-Human Assemblages of Children's Storytelling*. Dissertations and Theses. Paper 5445.

Myers, C. Y. (2017). Whatever we make depends: Doing-data/Data-doing with Young Children. In M. Koro-Ljungberg, T. Löytönen, & M. Tesar (Eds.), *Disrupting Data in Qualitative Inquiry: Entanglements with the Post-Critical and Post-Anthropocentric* (pp. 185–96). New York: Peter Lang.

Myers, C. Y. (2019). *Children and Materialities: The Force of the More-Than-Human in Children's Classroom Lives*. Singapore: Springer Nature.

Pink, S. (2013). *Doing Visual Ethnography*. Thousand Oaks, CA: Sage.

St. Pierre, E. A. (2011). Post qualitative research: The critique and the coming after. In N. K. Denzin & Y. S. Lincoln (Eds.), *Handbook of Qualitative Research* (4th ed., pp. 611–25). Thousand Oaks, CA: Sage.

2

Observing-without-reading; material attractions to stone and water

Abigail Hackett* and Christina MacRae**
Sheffield Hallam University
**Manchester Metropolitan University*

In this chapter, we take up MacRae and MacLure's (2021) invitation to seek out ways to connect with the experience of being a young child without reading this experience according to dominant systems of meanings. We do this as a way of grappling with our concerns around relying primarily on what we, as researchers, are able to perceive and record, when doing research with young children. To explore where this thread might lead us, we think with two events that took place in our recent research projects. Both of these involve young children in learning spaces; a child's play in a puddle outside a nursery and an encounter between a child and a piece of ironstone in a museum. We use these two events as a kind of thought experiment in attempting to 'see without reading' (MacRae & MacLure, 2021). Our aim is to explore the possibilities of an eye that

> tries to avoid subjecting participants – human and non-human, virtual and actual – to observation's ambition to comprehend; to circumscribe and bestow meaning.
>
> (MacRae & MacLure, 2021, p. 267)

The task here is to resist making sense of the child, but instead, through the sensing of matter, to find ways of foregrounding how more-than-human dimensions of events we witness can animate us as researchers rather than explaining child behaviour. In this we will explore approaches that prioritize what cannot be seen with the human eye; haptic felt-sense, atmospheres and the alternative timescales and relationalities (commonalities) accentuated by stone and water (both elements that feature in the events).

In previous thinking, we have both struggled with trying to mitigate against the effects of the construction of subjects as distinct from objects through the God-trick of the distancing practices of observation (MacRae, unpublished; Tesar et al., 2021), explored how our observation practices are already shaped by our ways of knowing (Jones et al., 2010) and aspired to interrupt habitual ways of seeing through defamiliarization and bringing to the surface the sticky data that forces us to think anew (MacRae et al., 2018). We orient ourselves very briefly by referring to some of the specific problematics related to dominant ways of observing children. Walkerdine draws from Foucault to give an account of the central role of observation in producing '"the child" as an object both of science in its own right and of the apparatuses of normalisation' (1984, p. 165). Following on from a long-standing approach to natural history, she goes on to trace how the discipline of child observation has been based on the principles of a rigorous classification and empirically verifiable gathering of facts that are read in relation to the science of child development. Emerging in the context of the nineteenth century, this approach went beyond the grouping of aspects of observed nature and was concerned with underlying orders of evolutionary progress and hierarchies of knowledge. She charts how child observation becomes a site where 'science and a pedagogy based on a model of naturally occurring development [] could be observed, normalised and regulated' (Walkerdine, 1984, p. 176). It is within this 'scientization of the child' (*ibid*, p. 171) already well under way, that Walkerdine traces how this paves the way for child observation to become a tool that also naturalizes pedagogy. Thus, child observation can be seen as 'a technology of normalisation, related to constructions of the child as nature and as reproducer of knowledge' (Dahlberg et al., 1999, p. 146).

The revelatory impulse that can be traced through observation can be linked with a will to grasp and to understand the Other (Viruru, 2001); 'the West moistens everything with meaning, like an authoritarian religion which imposes baptism on entire peoples' (Barthes, quoted by Trinh, 1991, p. 50). Making children's learning visible is never innocent, it reads meaning making into their activity, so that practices of surveillance, elicitation and documentation constrain behaviour precisely by 'making it more thoroughly knowable or known' (Rouse, on Foucault, 2005, p. 99). Reminding ourselves about the history of child observation reminds us that it is a practice that is perpetually in a state of being re-written, and that how we read observations is always a shifting site of interpretation. Yet at the same time traces of previous inscriptions always haunt more current observational practices.

In our experiment into trying to observe-without-reading, we are not claiming that we can escape the epistemological orders of knowledge that are impressed on how we see the world. Instead, we are interested in seeking ways of seeing that could perhaps change how we see children, rather than a quest to better see the child. Viruru (2001) draws our attention to how the

> the concept of understanding colonizes children since it assumes that they are transparent enough to be understood ... we deny them the right to be 'opaque', and insist that they become transparent, so that we might on the surface 'understand' them better, but essentially, control them more and more.
>
> (p. 38)

In using the term 'opacity', Viruru draws on the work of Edouard Glissant. Glissant uses the idea of opacity as a way to 'resist colonising tendencies, a distraction from absolute truths whose guardian I might believe myself to be' (1997, p. 192). He asks us to seek ways to relate to different others, but without *understanding* them, asking can we 'conceive of the opacity of the other of me, without reproach for my opacity for him?' (*ibid*, p. 193). He goes on to suggest that to feel solidarity with another, to build with another and to like what another does, it is not necessary for us to grasp *them*. In this chapter we ask ourselves what happens when we take up Viruru's challenge to resist observing children to understand them better, but instead to register something we feel that is sensed beyond our compulsion to interpret and comprehend. We are inspired by MacLure's (2021) concept of a divinatory methodology that engages with the 'queer temporality and spatiality of the Event' and that entertains 'forms of relation and participation that are always to some extent inhuman' (p. 510).

Reconsidering an observation of a child with stone (Abi)

A two-year-old boy runs down the museum corridor. His legs move so fast I am unsure his feet will keep up. The alternating colours of the striped corridor carpet flash by as I follow his line of movement. He stops abruptly at the end of the corridor, where a large piece of ironstone, bigger than the boy, sits on open display. It's grey surface shimmers with rainbow minerals inside it. He gazes at the surface of the ironstone and places the palm of his hand flat against its bulky surface.

In my telling of this memory of an incident during some fieldwork, a small child is characterized by movement and (perhaps) wonder or interest is alluded to, as he encounters a large museum object, which seems characterized by its permanence and enduring nature. As Springgay and Truman (2016) point out, rocks are generally seen anthropocentrically, both as inert and in terms of their use value to humans. This is indeed frequently the case in museum collections, where objects are accessioned according to agreed collecting policies; in the case of local museums, the collecting policy often centres on the significance of the object to people from that local area. The ironstone on display in this museum was considered important and relevant for the museum collections because it is an example of the high-lime content ironstone on which the town is situated. The town in fact came into the existence during the nineteenth century as a result of the ironstone geology; once iron ore was 'rediscovered' in the area by local landowners, iron works, mines and steel works were established. In both museum and early childhood spaces, objects are frequently codified according to, for example, the information they are intended to convey to the visitor (Dudley, 2010) or the learning they are supposed to make available to the child (Boomer, 2003). From that perspective, the ironstone is there to signify to the visitor something about the geology and history of the local area, perhaps connected in some way with their own sense of identity or local belonging.

In my mind's-eye, I return to the small boy pressing his hand against the ironstone. There will have been a label next to the exhibit, drawing visitors' attention to the significance of ironstone for the town. The boy looks happy and engaged, although he is not old enough to be interested in the relevance of ironstone to the local heritage. Instead, he makes sense of the museum by moving through it, engaging equally with the stairs, furniture, lighting and windows that frequently captivate young children in museums spaces (Hackett et al., 2018), as well as certain objects and cases that make up the museum collection itself. Wallis and Noble (2022) describe a relationship between children's movement through and in the museum and their sense of belonging in the space, arguing that children enter into dialogue with the building through traces, movement and mark making, as a way of developing a sense of belonging and ownership in cultural settings. This is a different kind of scenario to the one described in the paragraph above; rather than seeing objects and knowing the information about their relevance as a path to connection and belonging, fleeting movement and gesture via 'footprints and pathways that the children (re)create, depict, extend and continue the dialogue with the museum space' (Wallis & Noble, 2022), enabling and attending to children's preferred modes of making sense of the space. Yet through these modes of meaning making, often preferred by young children, 'meanings can solidify or slip-slide out of view again' (Hackett, 2021, p. 154); observing children's learning/engagement via these kinds of modes creates uncertainty and questions, rather than evidence to buttress the observer's position and conclusions. Rather than viewing this as an inconvenience, or a methodological glitch to be erased (MacLure, 2013), in this chapter I consider the provisionality of what a child might *mean* when belonging, desire and energy are expressed through the body with few words, as an invitation to observing-without-reading.

Community biographies, atmospheres and unspoken stories (Abi)

Without the ironstone, this area would have been rural, rather than an industrial town; as a 'monotown' (a town relying economically primarily on one industry), communities here have been vulnerable to shifts in demand and profitability of iron and steel, as global economies have faltered or production moved overseas, for example. As the boy moves down the corridor, the mums on this museum visit walk behind, chatting, about their local area, and how it was recently featured on a TV documentary 'Skint', one of an increasing number of 'poverty porn' documentaries that profile the lives and difficulties of those living in underserved communities or on low incomes. The families are very clear that their community was 'set up' by the documentary makers, who sought out extreme stories and, they tell me, paid young people to be filmed riding their bikes in a threatening manner around the estate.

There are so many things at play in this moment: the boy running down a corridor, the steel-working history, the families' critique of 'poverty porn', the small chubby palm pressing onto the museum exhibit, the neat Perspex stand and carefully written exhibit label, the way in which families express so eloquently their frustration and feelings of powerlessness to resist 'damage centred narratives' (Tuck, 2009) about their lives and their places. These things all hover in the air, yet it is hard to join up the dots. My brief in this research was to look at how children experience the museum, what they learn and how the museum could develop its spaces to better cater for this audience. As Jones et al. (2014) have pointed out, in order to draw confident conclusions about what is happening and why, there is often a need in early childhood research to strip down, simplify and look for what can be observed and how a meaning can be convincingly attached to it.

> Complexity, the 'thick of things', is not only lost, it becomes fundamentally threatening as it undermines the imposing edifices constructed from comparative data.
>
> (Jones et al., 2014, p. 64)

Here, this kind of straightforward observing-then-reading would assess the boy's engagement with the exhibit and then seek any evidence of connection between the intended significance of the exhibit (local geology, and its relevance to local heritage and life in the past/present) and the boy's understanding. Finding little there, such a practice of observing-then-reading might instead fall back onto an explanation of future intended benefits (supposing, for example, that creating museum-loving young children now will lead to museum advocates who appreciate their local heritage later).

Reconsidering a (non)observation of a puddle-jumping event (Christina)

In this section, the focus shifts from child/stone encounters in a museum to child/water encounters in a nursery outdoor space. I offer this event to keep to our shared question of *how can we see without reading?* I was struck by Abi's use of the phrase 'in my mind's-eye' and it recalled an event that has equally produced an image in my mind's-eye from a recent research project. The image that was conjured for me was of a child making a big splash in a puddle, having jumped off a climbing frame. This was an event that was recounted to me over zoom during lockdown by the early years practitioner (Shaffan) in whose classroom I was supposed to have been carrying out fieldwork. Because of the Covid-19 pandemic I found myself instead communicating via e-mails and zoom calls as I was not permitted to go into the school itself because of social distancing regulations. During this point of the pandemic, only the children of essential keyworkers were attending nursery school, and children were grouped into one room rather than according to age. To minimize viral transmission children spent as much time as possible outside.

During one of my zoom conversations Shaffan narrated with excitement and pleasure how much fun the children had been having jumping into puddles after a heavy period of rain. She spoke about how a heavy downpour had led to a section of astro-turf pooling into a large puddle, and how a child had started to launch themself from a nearby climbing structure into the puddle. This instance has possibly particularly niggled at me, as I was not 'actually' there, but still it produced a strong mind's-eye image that was full of vitality and movement: somehow this is unsettling. It confronted me with a realization about my need, as a researcher, for the authenticity of the actual instance that I had documented as data. Putting this under suspicion undoes some of my long-held efforts to make careful situated phenomenological observations (and perhaps in the need for data at all). These practices of archiving actuality are ones that I have invested much time in, both as a former nursery teacher and in my current position as a researcher.

So here, I am interested in trying to think of this child/puddle assembly that exists in my mind's-eye in general and universal terms rather than within the context of the situated child. This means that I must try and give up my tendencies to try to explain or understand *why* an individual child is compelled to jump and *what* the import of this is in terms of a child-facing pedagogy. This is work that goes against the grain, and yet it feels important that I try because of the way this child-puddle image resonates way beyond the actual instance (as does an image of a child running in a museum corridor). A child jumping in puddles is a ubiquitous and commonly held image: I only need to enter child/puddle into a web-based search engine to see how child/puddle images circulate in the virtual world of social media. It is not only that children are commonly drawn to bodies of water, but also that there is something that adults find irresistible about these moments which means that they proliferate and circulate. Thus, whilst each of the child/puddle encounters is birthed from the situated locale of the particularity of a child body and a puddle body (both bodies constituted in different proportions by water) – if we read this transversally, we can see 'the connections and unexpected openings situated knowledges make possible' (Haraway, 1988, p. 590).

Water: Thinking-in-movement? (Christina)

Following Pacini-Ketchabaw and Clark (2016), I wonder what else might I be able to see in this mind's-eye image of child/puddle if I try instead to 'think with water' (p. 99)? What might I notice if I attend to what Neimanis (2013) calls the hydro-logics of water and the way that a body of water moves? I will very briefly open up a few lines of thought that might take flight if I bring my focus to how the puddle water moves in response to the child, and the physics of the splash. When two small feet make contact with the surface of a puddle, a 'crown splash' is produced. The dynamics of the splash are so complex they do not follow predictable laws. It is this very complexity that makes puddles historically one of the main fascinations of fluid mechanics (Deggan et al., 2007). Physics scholars interested in fluid dynamics find that while there are observable regularities in the symmetry exhibited by the corona shaped splash that extend outwards from the point of water impact, the rim and the peaks of this crown are in a state of perpetual and unpredictable change. The cylindrical symmetry is a regularity that is always in a state of decomposition in relation to instabilities of wavelength and drops that break off from the end of each jet, producing droplets that further introduce non-linear instability (*ibid*). So, there is something here that I could perhaps tune into about the ways that 'water is always becoming' within the parameters of endless possibility. At the same time 'it is always seeking out differentiation, even in its brute materiality, one might say, [it] seemingly repeats' (Neimanis, 2009, p. 165). I am reminded that water's movement always escapes human capture – even if, in the context of the early years classroom, it predominantly figures as a resource to be 'managed' in relation to what learning outcomes it might yield (Pacini-Ketchabaw & Clark, 2016, p. 99).

What if instead of reading the child, I ask what might children have in common with water? Pacini-Ketchabaw and Clark (2016) suggest if we take up Neimanis's curiosity about water itself, this could offer new ways to approach the subjectivity of children. For example, what if I focus on the pooling qualities of all watery bodies, not just the pooling dimensions of puddles? This makes me wonder about the never settled quality of a pool of water since all bodies of water are prone to leaking and evaporation. At the same time, water attracts water by pooling and this gestures to a collective orientation. When Neimanis notes that water bodies always 'seek confluence' and 'flow into one another in life-giving ways, but also in unwelcome, or unstoppable, incursions' (2017, p. 29), perhaps this could help me to refigure child as also a body of water. This helps me to refigure children's situated knowledge as being 'about communities, not about isolated individuals' (Haraway, 1988, p. 590).

Reading mind's-eye images transcorporeally as queer archives

As we discuss together the idea of the mind's-eye, we notice how invested we often are, as researchers and educators, in *being there*, and the specificity and accuracy of observing what *this particular* child does in *this particular* moment, in order to read for meaning and implications. We both have seen a child play in water, or explore a museum, or touch something that interests them, or jump for fun, so many times. In our mind's-eye, just as in the search engine Christina mentions above, we imagine an archive of thematically similar images. A hundred moments of a child's legs pounding around a space. A thousand snapshots of a child's feet meeting a puddle. Each both generic and particular: (extra)ordinary. This is our archive of experiences, memories, stories and imaginings we draw on and recount when we write about children and learning.

Abi picks up on Christina's lament of not 'actually being there' during the puddle jumping incident, to reflect back on her own story of the boy and the piece of ironstone. It is a memory and a story to tell, squeezed through various iterations as time passes, publications from the research emerge and this one particular short incident, continues to stickily (MacRae et al., 2018) remain. Yes, Abi was there when that boy ran down that corridor. She observed with her own eyes as he pressed his small hand onto the ironstone. Does this matter? What difference does this make? Or to ask a more searching question, what difference does this mattering, this preference for 'real' and 'accurate' observations that can be repeated, described and read for meaning, produce, over time and in our collective imaginations?

Like museum collections, archives are typically collated according to a collecting policy and rules, with an attention to logic and completeness. In this sense,

> The archive is a place of order ruled by inert, naturalized, and detached values that relegates feelings and experiences that that cannot be documented easily to oblivion.
> (Danbolt, Rowley & Wolthers in Springgay & Truman, 2016, p.859)

Similarly, observations of individual children, when made with an emphasis on detail and specificity, and recorded alongside a clear reading of the significance and meaning of what has been observed, enact a version of childhood that is capable of being interpreted, in which each moment exemplifies the child's intent according to a rational function or desire. Next steps to continue intended learning or development on an upwards trajectory are thus assumed to present themselves in a straightforward way. Like a traditional archive, observing-for-reading creates an archive of observations of children that are 'closed and limited, fulfils a scientific need, and its value is determined by normative historical or research truths' (Springgay & Truman, 2016, p. 859).

Drawing on Cvetkovich's notion of a queer archive, Springgay and Truman (2016) consider the ways in which rocks can be considered an archive of geological history. Although rocks are often considered a chronological record of deep time, this is illusionary – in practice 'rocks erode, melt, collapse, and invert' (p. 861). This offers a possible starting point for conceptualizing our own observations of children as a queer archive of feeling (*ibid*), rather than a coherent and accumulating body of expertise. A queer archive, as proposed by Cvetkovich (2003), has different principles for selection and inclusion, it resists coherence in favour of fragmentation; it follows an archiving practice that is illogical where documents represent far more than the literal value of the objects themselves.

(Springgay & Truman, 2016, p. 860)

Rather than completeness, coherence and certainty, a queer archive is 'a form of counter-knowledge production' (*ibid*, p. 860). Inspired by the queer archive we become aware of what gets lost when we observe-then-read children, because when events take place that are 'not visible, given to documentation or sonic recording, or otherwise housable within an archive', they are lost' (Schneider, in Springgay & Truman, 2016, p. 860). We ask ourselves (again), 'what if'? What if we set out to create a queer archive: collections of found videos of children in puddles, illegible sounds (from a human perspective) and fragments of data that were not housable and did not fit within accepted pedagogical practices or qualitative research models grounded in validity and reliability? With a certain heavy-ness, we realize how much our research engagements and data collecting practices continue to centre and colonize the lives of children.

Concluding section

This chapter has been a conversation in which we made a commitment to ourselves (two early childhood researchers) to see children without reading them, and to think collaboratively with each other. Our aspiration has been to begin to delineate how paying attention to images held in our mind's-eye could become a way to productively unsettle the strangle-hold of observation as a practice of close noticing and swift reading for meaning. We wonder what thinking of these universal mind's-eye views of children with stone/water might do to further help us resist reading children through such literal observation. We hope that these universalist images we hold in our mind's-eye can be used to 'cultivate ways of imagining our lived experience as decentred, if always transcorporeally implicated' (Neimanis, 2017, p. 42).

Returning to the vignette of a child who presses their palm against a piece of ironstone, we are reminded by Springgay and Truman (2016) that 'stones are only inert when considered anthropocentrically' (p. 857), prompting us to ask what might be possible if we instead attend to that which we are unable to observe with the human eye; 'rocks' ability to move, quiver, and reproduce' (*ibid*, p. 852). The mind's-eye (rather than the naked-eye) image of the child and ironstone also yielded classed and gendered histories that hovered in the air circulating haunting and infected current reality TV depictions of the community who live there. None of these geo-logics are consciously at play in the child's compulsion to move towards the rock, but they are still dimensions of the event that matter. Moreover, the ironstone also clearly matters to the child: the ironstone extends an invitation, even if this is not anything to do with past histories that haunt present-day lives.

In a similar way, if we observe-then-read the child jumping in the puddle, then perhaps we focus on what they intended, or what they were learning. However, by focusing our attention to this human-centric mattering, we all too easily underestimate the multi-form qualities of water and the extent to which we humans (child or adult) are also watery bodies. We also lose out on what we might learn from children's relationship with the more-than-human world. If we shift our gaze to the matter that matters to children, instead of reading children, we might perhaps simply engage more with the matter at hand, and where the energy is flowing – not as something we can observe, but as something we can sense. When we tune more into these material attractions, perhaps we also realize there are things that we also already know in our mind's-eye, and that is why they leave such strong traces; they are not ways of knowing that we can name, but we are intimately familiar with them all the same.

The conversations that we have had in the writing of this chapter have drawn our attention to the risks that are involved when we site/sight children as bounded entities at the centre of our vision. Haraway tells us that,

> Boundaries are drawn by mapping practices; 'objects' do not pre-exist as such. Objects are boundary projects. But boundaries shift from within; boundaries are very tricky. What boundaries provisionally contain remains generative, productive of meanings and bodies. Siting (sighting) boundaries is a risky practice.
>
> (Haraway, 1988, p. 595)

What we have learnt from our conversation is that the material attractions of both stone and water can teach us precisely about the riskiness of siting (sighting) when we observe children. As substance both water and stone resist siting (sighting) because of the degree to which they are able to ultimately escape our human 'taxonomic efforts' (Neimanis, 2017a, p. 55), and this unknowability 'necessarily rejects total knowledge by any body' (*ibid*, p. 57). We realize that stopping ourselves from observing-then-reading is not a simple matter, as that is how we have learnt ourselves as Western, white, educated adults, to be human. However, by experimenting with our siting (sighting) practices then perhaps we can become more aware of our human worldly engagement rather than separating ourselves, or the children we see, from it.

References

Bomer, R. (2003). Things that make kids smart: A Vygotskian perspective on concrete tool use in primary literacy classrooms. *Journal of Early Childhood Literacy, 3*(3), 223–47.

Cvetkovich, A. (2003). *An Archive of Feelings Trauma, Sexuality, and Lesbian Public Cultures*. Durham: Duke University Press.

Dahlberg, G., Moss, P., & Pence, A. (1999). *Beyond Quality in Early Childhood Education and Care*. London: Falmer Press.

Danbolt, M., Wolthers, L., & Rowley, J. (Ed.) (2009). *Lost and Found: Queerying the Archive*. Kopenhagen: Kunsthallen Nikolaj.

Deegan, R. D., Brunet, P., & Eggers, J. (2007). Complexities of splashing. *Nonlinearity, 21*(1), C1.

Dudley, S. (Ed.) (2010). *Museum Materialities Objects, Engagements, Interpretation*. London: Routledge.

Glissant, E. (1997). *Poetics of Relation*. Michigan: University of Michigan Press.

Hackett, A. (2021). *More Than Human Literacies in Early Childhood*. London: Bloomsbury.

Hackett, A. Holmes, R. Macrae, C., & Procter, L. (2018). Young children's museum geographies; spatial, material and bodily ways of knowing. *Children's Geographies, 16*(5), 481–8.

Haraway, D. (1988). Situated knowledges: The science question in feminism and the privilege of partial perspective. *Feminist Studies, 14*(3), 575–99.

Jones, L., MacRae, C., Holmes, R., & MacLure, M. (2010). Documenting classroom life: How can I write about what I am seeing? *Qualitative Research*, *10*(4), 479–91.

Jones, L., Osgood, J., Holmes, R., & MacLure, M. (2014). (Re)assembling, (Re)casting and (Re)aligning Lines of De- and Re-Territorialisation of early childhood. *International Review of Qualitative Research*, *7*(1), 58–79.

Leal, B. (2005). Childhood between literature and philosophy. Readings of childhood in manoel de barros' poetry. *Childhood and Philosophy*, *1*(1), 111–24.

MacRae, C. (2008). *Making Space: Organising, Representing and Producing Space in the Early Years Classroom*. unpublished thesis.

MacRae, C., Hackett, A., Holmes, R., & Jones, L. (2018). Vibrancy, repetition, movement: Posthuman theories for reconceptualising young children in museums. *Children's Geographies*, *16*(5), 503–15.

MacRae, C. & MacLure, M. (2021). Watching two-year-olds jump: Video method becomes 'haptic'. *Ethnography and Education*, *16*(3), 263–78.

MacLure, M. (2013). Researching without representation? Language and materiality in post-qualitative methodology. *International Journal of Qualitative Studies in Education*, *26*(6), 658–67.

MacLure, M. (2021). Inquiry as divination. *Qualitative Inquiry*, *27*(5), 502–11.

Neimanis, A. (2009). Bodies of water, human rights and the hydrocommons. *TOPIA: Canadian Journal of Cultural Studies*, *21*, 161–82. https://doi.org/10.3138/topia.21.161%5D.

Neimanis, A. (2013). Feminist subjectivity, watered. *Feminist Review*, *103*(1), 23–41.

Neimanis, A. (2017a). Embodying water: Feminist phenomenology for posthuman worlds. In *Bodies of Water: Posthuman Feminist Phenomenology* (pp. 27–64). London: Bloomsbury Academic.

Neimanis, A. (2017b). Water and knowledge. In D. Christian & R. Wong (Eds.), *Downstream: Reimagining Water* (pp. 51–68). Ontario: Wilfrid Laurier University.

Pacini-Ketchabaw, V. & Clark, V. (2016). Following watery relations in early childhood pedagogies. *Journal of Early Childhood Research 14*(1), 98–111.

Rouse, J. (2005). Power/Knowledge. In G. Gutting (Ed.), *Cambridge Companion to Foucault"*. Cambridge: Cambridge University Press.

Springgay, S. & Truman, S. E. (2016). Stone Walks: inhuman animacies and queer archives of feeling. *Discourse: Studies in the Cultural Politics of Education*, *38*(6), 851–63.

Tesar, M., Duhn, I., Nordstrom, S., Koro, M., Sparrman, A. et al. (2021). Infantmethodologies. *Educational Philosophy and Theory*. Online first. DOI: 00131857.2021.2009340.

Trinh, T. Minh-ha (1991). *When the Moon Waxes Red*. London: Routledge.

Tuck, E. (2009). Suspending damages: A letter to communities. *Harvard Educational Review, 79*, 409–27.

Viruru, R. (2001). Colonized through Language: the case of early childhood education. *Contemporary Issues in Early Childhood, 2*(1), 31–47.

Walkerdine, V. (1984). Developmental Psychology and the child-centred pedagogy: The insertion of Piaget into early education. In J. Henriques, W. Holloway, C. Urwin, & V. Walkerdine (Eds.), *Changing the Subject*. London: Methuen.

Wallis, N. & Noble, K. (2022). Leave only footprints: How children communicate a sense of ownership and belonging in an art gallery, *European Early Childhood Education Research Journal*, Online first. DOI: 10.1080/1350293X.2022.2055100.

3

Down on the ground: The material memoir of the posthuman childhood researcher

Jayne Osgood
Middlesex University

Tracing affective forces in childhood research

As I set about writing a contribution to a book about postdevelopmental approaches to research observation in childhood studies I observe, or rather I sense, that this is a practice that has profoundly shifted over many years of undertaking research and yet also remained comfortably familiar. I began by gathering memories and artefacts from the numerous times I have been in early childhood contexts: nurseries, children's centres, family homes, libraries, playgrounds, parks; and to ponder upon the various ways that observation has been framed, permitted and at times denied or subverted. I am struck by research as a series of embodied affective forces; and by how theories and philosophies shape worldviews and ways of being so that moments 'captured' through observation in early childhood contexts become endlessly fascinating, troubling and lively when encountered from different onto-epistemological starting points. Observations agitate and provoke; they have capacities to activate a deep contemplation of how it might be possible to find ways to live on a damaged planet (Tsing, 2015). Furthermore, observations transport the researcher through embodied, affective forces to times forgotten; research encounters become etched upon the researcher body and agitate a series of atmospheric attunements that take the research beyond the specific early childhood context and allow childhood to be thought of as processes that are worldly and confederate. The research ceases to be about observing what children can do, or what their actions might mean instead it can become an opening or what Stewart (2007) terms a contact zone where connections, routes and disjunctures can be mapped.

The children and babies featured in my research over the years are curiously fixed in time and space in fieldwork observations either as notes, scribbles, photographs or video footage, but their liveliness lingers and resurfaces in unexpected ways. Revisiting these observations, I am provoked by the messy, emergent, untameable, discomforts and joys of researching in early childhood that resurface to agitate memories: I am reminded of where I lived, the clothes I wore, of pregnancies, bereavements, of 9/11, Grenfell Tower, medical diagnoses and Covid-19. I am taken back to glimpses of my own childhood and those of my own children. As I catch sight of my hand, or foot, hear my voice, sense my presence in those observations I am reminded of Code (2006, p. 4) and her insistence for ecological thinking in research practices, which:

> relocates inquiry down on the ground where knowledge is made, negotiated, circulated, and which proposes a way of engaging with the implications of patterns, places, and the interconnections of lives and events in and across the human and non-human world in scientific and secular projects of inquiry.

Most of my research has indeed been 'down on the ground', characterized by a messy tapestry of bodies, matter, affective forces, policy documents, curriculum frameworks, snot, tears, sand, all within a swirling landscape full of both familiarity and strangeness. As the years have passed, I have become ever more attuned to an ecological way of thinking about and undertaking research, and with a deep commitment to feminist new materialism I now embrace irruptions, haltings and disorientations (Koro Lungberg, 2015) as generative of fresh optics with which to grapple with the world, and as offering capacities for ethical world-making through research. As a result, increasingly the research I undertake to contribute to debates in early childhood looks unrecognizable when mapped against research methods handbooks. But it is my contention that attuning to atmospheric affects (Stewart, 2011) is generative of a deeper, more nuanced account of childhood in the Anthropocene.

In this chapter, I revisit and weave selected research observations with young children from over the past twenty years. In doing this, I seek to disrupt established ideas about the practice of observation as a research methodology.

Following Alaimo (2010, 2016), I want to argue that all bodies (human and non-human) are shaped by environments; that transformation is constantly occurring in response to surroundings and that history is being registered on, in and through bodies. She contends that there is never a time when humans can be anything but transcorporeal. Making use of the material memoir involves tracing bodily immersion within power structures that have real material effects – I therefore take research observations as opportunities for such tracings. With the help of Alaimo's concept of transcorporeality and Stewart's (2007, 2011) ordinary affects and atmospheric attunements, this chapter tunes in to forces, absent-presences, memories and hauntings to argue that observations have capacities to re-turn us to times forgotten, transport us to other entirely unanticipated places and to pose deeply political questions long after 'data' is 'collected'. Understanding research observation as more than a method for gathering data and making meaning of what has been witnessed involves a recognition inspired by feminist new materialism that research is always a deeply embodied, material-affective, political practice.

Queering observation in early childhood

As stressed (and variously contested) throughout this book, observation in childhood research is typically associated with what can be seen and registered. It is concerned with collecting data to extract some form of representational knowledge about the developing child. There is a long and varied history of using child observations to further understandings of child development and education (see MacNaughton et al., 2001 for a detailed overview). It is important for the purposes of this chapter though to note that observations are always shaped by the epistemological orientation of the researcher and how they come to define what counts as valid knowledge (Lather, 1993). In early childhood research a variety of observation methods exist from highly structured approaches that view the early childhood context as some form of laboratory for extracting evidence and making truth claims; to more naturalistic approaches where the researcher becomes more deeply immersed in the environment and relationships that unfold over time and is more open to what unfolds. Regardless of where a researcher sits along this continuum the focus is most typically on the child and tends towards an anthropocentric logic. Researchers become accustomed to making sense of what is seen; what observations can tell us about the child, in the moment, against some narrow imaginary of the developmental child. Feminist new materialist and post-humanist approaches though encourage researchers to question the logic of focusing solely or most intently upon the child in childhood research. Rather the concern becomes to trouble taken-for-granted assumptions by dwelling upon relationalities and what emerges through encounters, being open to surprises and recognizing our infected and affected intertwinement with that which we are researching; a recognition and celebration of what Haraway (1988) terms 'situated knowledges' and 'partial perspectives'. The researcher becomes a 'mutated modest witness' (see Osgood, 2019 for fuller discussion) by making use of the personal, political, activist baggage she brings to the research. Being explicit about who we are as researchers, the agendas that underpin our feminist, anti-bias, social justice driven projects is now much more readily accepted in early childhood research. I have become increasingly more resolute in making this completely transparent in my research as the years have gone by.

Fabricating a material memoir of the feminist researcher

Thinking back to studies that I have undertaken where observation is a core methodology, I arrive back to the early 2000s and specifically my doctoral research. In my late twenties, with several years as a jobbing researcher under my belt, I was eager to undertake research with an unapologetically political agenda: to hear the voices of working-class women 'down on the ground' with young children. This involved extensive critique of government policy, interviews with national stakeholders and localized ethnographic work in three London nurseries. Talking methodologies: interviews and focus groups were privileged but as the research visits unfolded, I found myself undertaking something of an 'accidental ethnography' with the inclusion of extensive observations of daily life at the nurseries.

Endless visits to the nurseries involved prolonged waiting around for staff to be available to participate in life history interviews. I spent many hours sitting patiently in either the staff room, book corner, the playground, the manager's office; or wherever else I was told to wait. This positioning made it impossible *not* to attune to the daily life that was unfolding around me, as I cast an eye back over my fieldwork diary, I can see that some of the richest and affecting data was generated from this accidental method. The observations were entirely unstructured, not in search of anything in particular, just soaking up the atmosphere, the tempo, the environment, the comings and goings. At the time I remember feeling quite anxious that I would be denied opportunities to collect the data I had come for, i.e. the interview recordings, but I came to unexpectedly enjoy simply hanging around. My fieldnotes attend to smells, weather, sticky surfaces, atmospheric tensions.

One prolonged entry dwells upon a book I happened upon whilst being parked in book corner for over two hours. I am troubled by what appears to be snot and bogies adhered to the covers of a book that is torn and has battered pages. Curiously I appear not have made a note of the title of the book, the story line, characters or plot. Rather it is the materiality of the book, its battered and infested state that arrests my attention and sends my thought processes in all sorts of random directions. Perhaps unsurprisingly, these observations do not make it into the thesis, but I do recall sharing them with my supervisors; how the microbes, dried nasal mucus and perhaps other bodily fluids decorating the exhausted book, had troubled me. An encounter with this book worked upon my (pre-maternal) young, (once) working-class body. It clearly agitated ordinary affects and left a lasting imprint as I now notice the care that I lavished upon my own children's picturebooks: wiping them clean, fixing, gluing, sewing and preserving them, for what I am not entirely sure. That dishevelled picturebook in book corner, Mulberry Bush nursery; an underfunded, voluntary sector nursery nestled within a deprived housing estate in north London, brought to life embodied senses of social class and complex processes of social mobility: a working-class girl from the village, first generation to university, then a doctoral student and now, a professor, a mother. Hauntings of that book and its connections to picturebooks stashed on my children's bookshelves agitate memories of the near empty bookshelf of my childhood home (with the notable exception of *Mrs Beaton's Book of Household Management, Gideons Bible, The Gardener's Year* and half a dozen *Reader's Digests*).

The picture book and its hauntings, the vital materialism (Bennett, 2010) of what it was, how it lives on in ways that I could not have anticipated, was at the time laughed away as inconsequential in a supervision meeting. We reasoned that my reaction was symptomatic of tendencies towards obsessive cleanliness, which I had attributed to heightened working-class respectability, as Skeggs (2003) writes about it. The squarely anthropocentric framing of my doctoral research meant that these irruptions and haltings, brought about by everyday affects, were dismissed as an irrelevance and distraction, I readjusted my lens to focus upon social class as a human, subjective and socially constructed concern that was contained within the immediate ethnographic context of my research. What does make its way into the thesis is a critical reflection about the out-of-placeness of my once working-class but upwardly mobile self:

> By revisiting my fieldnotes I can trace the considerable anxiety I experienced about my 'presentation of self', how I was being read, who was *I* to be undertaking *this* research? I was caught between feeling voyeuristic, an encumbrance; overly studious to, at other times, experiencing inclusion as 'one of the girls, down on the floor with the children' this was especially the case when I was invited to participate in the Summer Fete, and some months later, the Christmas Party. I continually reflected upon the fact that I was an outsider and the extent to which I was included rested upon a willingness to be accepted into the daily life of the nursery.
>
> (PhD Thesis, p. 61)

Looking back to these observations nearly two decades later I can appreciate the centrality of the researcher body, and specifically research as a series of embodied encounters that both affect and are affecting, long after the research is published. Thinking with the microbes and dried nasal mucus conjures the current Covid-19 pandemic and the increased precarity of the early years workforce (see Osgood, 2022 for a fuller discussion of this). Alaimo (2010) writes of the proletarian lung of the worker, where the nature of the work inscribes itself within the materiality of the body. On the frontline, early years workers persistently suffer bodily immersion within power structures that have very real material effects: handling toxic cleaning fluids; fatigue from long working hours; spinal problems from sitting on too small furniture, exhaustion from long commutes because they are priced out of local housing where nurseries are located, and now, acute and prolonged exposure to a deadly virus. Attuning to the seemingly unremarkable, taking seriously that which causes a stutter in our thinking, that which invites curiosity with ordinary affects, in fact holds the potential to open important ways to consider childhood research that break free from narrow constraints of what we *should* be observing and what it means. As Stewart (2007, p. 10) writes about tuning in:

> The ordinary is a circuit that's always tuned into something little, something somewhere. A mode of attending to the possible and the threatening, it amasses the resonance of things. It flows through cliches of the self, agency, home, a life. It pops up as a dream. Or it shows up in the middle of a derailing. Or in a simple pause. It can take flights of fancy or go limp, tired, done for now. It can pool up on the little worlds of identity and desire. It can draw danger. Or it can dissipate, leaving you standing.

Scripts etched on the body

Another study that floats to the surface when contemplating the embodied complexities of undertaking childhood research observations was that undertaken when I was mother to a young toddler. The research was concerned to explore how best to engage 'hard to reach' families in early years music-making (Osgood et al., 2013). A core method employed in the study was observation in several case study early years music-making services. As the study was externally funded by a national charity seeking to reform policy and make improvements to practice, there was a very clear set of aims and objectives to be addressed by gathering evidence from the field. Observations at the music sessions were structured by an observation schedule that directly corresponded to the aims and objectives of the study. The research team was in search of quite precise data about the level and nature of engagement of parents and young children.

However, as is frequently the case when 'down on the ground' in childhood studies the encounters quickly became characterized by porous boundaries and messy irruptions and entanglements. In all the research I have undertaken with young children and babies it has been impossible to sit at a distance, to be a dispassionate, objective observer (see Osgood, 2019, 2020 for recent examples). The observation guide is intended as boundary-setting apparatus but early childhood environments, and child improvisers, movers and shakers actively disrupt such frameworks. I am magnetically drawn into the otherworldliness of early childhood environments; opportunities to tune into children's explorations and resistances are irresistible. Inevitably I find myself on the ground, with my notebook either forgotten or in the possession of a small child. My researcher body assumes intuitive responses to the situation, in this particular moment my body responded to the affective forces that demanded 'engaged mother'; having participated in many Mini Mozart and Rhyme Times in the local library with my son, the script is etched upon my body. I am poised, punctual, keen, enthusiastic, there to scaffold a child's learning. I sense the rules of the game, the unspoken but explicit expectations. I sit crossed legged on the ground suspecting that I know what is to come. As childhood researcher I find ways to resist the script and instead tune in to the chaos and noise, attempting to remain open, to suspend judgement, or as Stewart (2007, p. 1) writes:

> Committed not to the demystification and uncovered truths that support a well-known picture of the world, but rather to speculation, curiosity, and the concrete, it tries to provoke attention to the forces that come into view as habit or shock, resonance or impact. *Something* throws itself together in a moment as an event and a sensation; a something both animated and inhabitable

… A 'something' that did not get published:

I sense a small body behind me
rummaging
through a parked buggy lined up against the wall
rustling
rummaging
a packet of <i>Space Invaders</i> is unearthed
a look around
rustling
rummaging
then a <i>Fruit Shoot</i>
another furtive glance around
a mother's blushed cheeks
The Wheels on the Bus signals the start

This 'something' set in motion all sorts of affective residues and tensions during the session, igniting class judgement, regulatory impulses and subversive satisfaction. Whilst we do not dwell upon this observation in the report (not least because it did fit into the neat boxes of the observation schedule) it nevertheless continues to resurface, to have a vitalism that lingers. Stewart (2007) stresses that 'a something' does not work through meanings, rather ordinary affects pick up density and texture as they move through bodies, dramas and social worldings of all kinds. She goes on to explain that their significance lies in the intensities that they build and the thoughts and feelings that they make possible. It is not so much whether this something is good or bad per se, rather the point is that it generates ways of knowing, relating, and attending to things that are already present in them, for how they resonate. We note the force of this 'something' and other, similar ordinary affects, in the report:

> The social class signifiers embodied in the music leader and her assistant had important affects in determining the appeal of the session and parental 'performances' which tended towards an implicit recognition of what was expected of them and their children (punctuality, active participation, adherence to unspoken rules). For example, consuming food during the sessions, roaming free and chatting were actively discouraged and were viewed as signalling disengagement and acting as a distraction.
>
> (Osgood et al., 2012, p. 50)

Now they could run around before it started,
then I would arrive,
I always started and finished the session with The Wheels on the Bus –
they knew it was starting
then they knew it was finished.
once it had started everybody had to sit still.
It wasn't playgroup
if one child starts to run, they all run
So, they all sat on mum's knees
or on the floor
But every so often
I would explain that letting them run around was spoiling it for everybody else
the idea was the children should concentrate

> *I mean it really becomes a discipline*
> *children learn what they need for school*
> *and of course*
> *culturally it was interesting*
> *big variations in how parents raise their children*
> *but they all accepted*
> *knew what was coming*
> *I just kept the momentum up*
> *once I started*
> *I didn't stop until the end*
>
> (Librarian cited in Osgood et al., 2013, pp. 51–2)

Not missing the everyday somethings

The everyday somethings that surface in early childhood contexts are at risk of being missed or dismissed altogether. They are rarely what researchers go in search of, yet they have the capacities to demand attention, to provoke curiosity, to tell different stories if we are open to registering affect. Tracing back through decades of research in search of the somethings that were erased, pushed aside but somehow resurface and demand fresh optics has been an invigorating exercise. Bringing the material self into the frame of research and contemplating how research is etched upon the body and the body etched upon the research feels like an imperative, as Alaimo (2010, p. 20) stresses:

> As the material self cannot be disentangled from networks that are simultaneously economic, political, cultural, scientific, and substantial, what was once the ostensibly bounded human subject finds herself in a swirling landscape of uncertainty where practices and actions that were once not remotely ethical or political suddenly become the very stuff of the crises at hand.

As I have become increasingly immersed in feminist new materialism and critical posthumanism these practices of noticing, attuning through embodied, affective encounters have become central. Observation has become something much more intuitive, sensory and speculative; indeed much more childlike in its receptivity to the curiousness of the world. Haraway's (1988) figure of the mutated modest witness has been especially helpful when seeking to further explore what else gets agitated when observation is freed from its epistemic, methodological straight jacket. Haraway (2016) urges that as mutated modest witnesses, researchers should engage in deep hanging out, to go visiting and to venture off the beaten path; heeding this advice results in surprising and at times discomforting research with children. As she states:

> The point is to make a difference in the world, to cast our lot from some ways of life and not others. To do that one must be in the action, be finite and dirty, not transcendent and clean.
>
> (Haraway, 1988, p. 36)

Observing the routine, everyday material discursive entanglements unfolding and enfolding within early childhood contexts creates space for other stories to emerge in unexpected and unanticipated ways. In recent publications (Osgood, 2019, 2020, 2022; Osgood et al., 2022), I recount strange encounters with routine and everyday happenings that interrupt and fracture the familiarity of being in a nursery, disrupting the predictability and easy recognition of the organization of space, furniture and materials. Taking up the figure of the mutated modest witness and exercising what Tsing (2015) terms 'the art of noticing' makes simple, mundane acts such as talking and sitting something else entirely. Research in this mode pushes bodies out of place, out of time, making them excessive, all of which creates possibilities to encounter early childhood with a completely different optics:

> The ordinary can turn on you … it can flip into something else altogether. One thing leads to another. An expectation is dashed or fulfilled. An ordinary floating state of things goes sour or takes off into something amazing and good. Either way, things turn out to be not what you thought they were … The ordinary is a thing that has to be imagined and inhabited.
>
> (Stewart, 2007, p. 105)

In this key, the childhood researcher is required to be open to the queerness that resides in spaces where habits, magic and fantasy comingle with regulation, containment and surveillance. Taking up an *Alice in Wonderland* sensibility (Nordstrom et al., 2018; Osgood, 2020), working with the affordances that discomfort, awkwardness, excess and being out of place generate provides a portal through which to unsettle established ideas about childhood. What counts as valid knowledge (Lather, 1993) and what counts as research (Rhedding-Jones, 2005) is called into sharp focus. Posthumanist inquiry becomes a part of everyday life: everything, everyone, everyplace, each little glimmer and snap has capacities to set off curiosity; provide tentacles to follow.

This researcherly self is not contained within nurseries or other bounded early years contexts. It becomes a way of life (Ferrando, 2012). Furthermore, this researcherly self can be understood as always in the making. Atmospheric attunements that hail attention today are informed by long buried nightmares and anxieties from childhood. Living very close to a nuclear weapons base[1] terror sat permanently in the pit of my stomach; afraid to open the fridge as invisible CFCs[2] escaped into the also invisible Ozone layer; shutting windows tight on hot summer days to keep out toxic fertilizers and pesticides[3] sprayed year after year on the fields surrounding my family home; charity fundraisers for the Amazonian deforestation[4]; Attenborough warning about species extinction; creatures (human and non-human) deformed by the Chernobyl disaster[5]; relativities of local[6] and global poverty, gender- and classed-based inequalities[7]; these childhood hauntings infuse and infect the materiality of the researcher body; they become reawakened and achingly familiar. Childhood research does not start and stop down on the ground in the nursery; it begins in our own childhoods, in our bones and sinews, and continues throughout the ebb and flow of our lives. The material self configures differently and intensifies as bodies are shaped, and in turn shape the world and its hauntings as we seek to make it a better place, through our research and everyday living.

(Im)possibilities of undertaking research with(out) children

The material memoir illustrates the ways that researching seeps into our pores, our psyches, our muscles and memories, we are always mutated modest witnesses, always affected and infected by that which we research. This has been acutely felt during endless months of being denied opportunities to physically hang out in early childhood contexts. Researching from the depths of a pandemic has insisted upon different optics, in search of alternative places to encounter childhood and contemplate how it is interwoven through space, histories and temporalities that manifest within chance encounters – for example, a walk in the park, an encounter with a nursery outing, lichen and a dead pigeon (Osgood, 2022).

During pandemic lockdown I happened upon an accidental walking method (op.cit); as modern-day Flâneuse, I became aware of previously unnoticed events and encounters that unfold in the everyday in-between spaces with sharpened senses ready to attune to sights, sounds and smells that seemed to demand close attention. Cuddles, tears and snotty noses, lichen, bacteria and liminal animals together populated a trip to the local park during hard lock-down, to offer a powerful account of inequality and precarity, that incited a stutter. Alaimo (2010, p. 28) asserts that one's body is 'never a rigidly enclosed, protected entity, but is vulnerable to the substances and flows of its environments'. She goes on to argue that humans and other animals are never separate and distinct from the environments and landscapes within which they exist, and in turn exist within them. I argue that the logics of capitalism determining the nature and availability of early childhood education is intricately bound up with the non- and more-than-human. I focus on lichen as story-teller and what the death of a pigeon during lockdown has to tell about multispecies survival in the Anthropocene to argue that we co-exist in a system of constantly interweaving subjectivities which can never be truly separated from each other. Or Tsing (2015, p. 20) asserts:

> Precarity is the condition of being vulnerable to others. Unpredictable encounters transform us; we are not in control, even of ourselves. Unable to rely on stable structure of community, we are thrown into shifting assemblages, which remake us as well as others.

Covid-19 has altered life in many ways including how childhood studies are conceived, undertaken and what they generate. The mode of research I am arguing for in this chapter enables the researcher to tap into what virusing-with (see Osgood et al, 2022) as method has to offer. It demands that researchers mobilize a deep attunement, to allow themselves to be affected and to wonder at what might be learnt or unlearnt from encountering deeply unsettling time in a portal (Roy, 2022). As childhood researchers, we are in the unique position to learn with and from 'child'. We might take seriously Manning's (2020, p. 6) claim that:

> child is a researcher of life, and a maker of worlds. The indefinite runs through the child, protecting it from the frames we so eagerly wish to impose on it. The becoming-child promises no return to an innocent beginning. There is no inner child. What there is, in every line, is an indeterminate tendency for resonating with what else moves across it. This is the becoming-child of the line.

Researching down on the ground

For Alaimo (2010) the material memoir is a form of trans-corporeal autobiography typically crafted by an author who has suffered illness. The author interprets the environment through the lens of her sickness, in search of its origin. Narratives of personal history, of local history, of science and of environment are drawn together in ways that imply an attribution. Therefore, material memoir is always a genre of doubt, of indeterminacy, of discourse that is speculative and inconclusive. In this chapter, I have made use of the material memoir as a framework to think about childhood research as etched upon the researcher body and how in turn the researcher body infuses research encounters. Tracing embodied encounters of the feminist researcher shaped by personal and local histories and life in late capitalism together with attuning to ordinary affects of the somethings that surface in childhood research hold the potential to recognize that our understandings are only ever partial and situated. Affective methodologies involve becoming attuned to what (else) a particular scene might offer, and they have the capacity to insist that we get down on the ground to embrace a more childlike approach to research.

Notes

1. A history of RAF Welford: https://www.greenhamcommon.org.uk/raf-welford.
2. Lasting impact of CFCs on the environment: https://eandt.theiet.org/content/articles/2020/03/old-fridges-found-to-be-leaking-ozone-destroying-cfcs/.

3   Cancer amongst agricultural communities: https://pubmed.ncbi.nlm.nih.gov/3294455/.
4   Save the Amazon Appeal: https://savingtheamazon.org/en.
5   Cancer inducing effects of nuclear disaster: https://chernobylguide.com/chernobyl_children.
6   Rural poverty, increased polarisation: https://www.jrf.org.uk/report/poverty-and-wealth-across-britain-1968-2005 https://www.newstatesman.com/politics/2017/02/how-uk-can-avoid-repeat-1980s-inequality.
    Global poverty, https://ourworldindata.org/extreme-poverty.
7   https://www.pinknews.co.uk/2021/11/18/what-was-section-28-law-lgbt/.

References

Alaimo, S. (2010). *Bodily Natures: Science, Environment and the Material Self*. Bloomington: Indiana University Press.

Alaimo, S. (2016). *Exposed: Environmental Politics and Pleasures in Posthuman Times*. Minneapolis: University of Minnesota Press.

Bennett, J. (2010). *Vibrant Matter: A Political Ecology of Things*. Durham: Duke University Press.

Code, L. (2006). *Ecological Thinking: The Politics of Epistemic Location*. Oxford: Oxford University Press.

Ferrando, F. (2012). Towards a posthumanist methodology. *A Statement Frame Journal for Literary Studies*, 25(1), 9–18.

Haraway, D. J. (2016). *Staying with the Trouble: Making Kin in the Chthulucene*. Durham: Duke University Press.

Haraway, D. J. (1988). Situated knowledges: The science question in feminism and the privilege of the partial perspective. *Feminist Studies*, 14(3), 575–99.

Koro-Ljungberg, M. (2015). *Reconceptualizing Qualitative Research: Methodologies without Methodology*. London: Sage.

Lather, P. (1993). Fertile obsession: Validity after poststructuralism. *The Sociological Quarterly*, 34(4), 673–93.

MacNaughton, B., Rolfe, S. A., & Siraj-Blatchford, I. (2001). *Doing Early Childhood Research: International Perspectives on Theory & Practice*. Milton Keynes: Open University Press.

Manning, E. (2020). Radical pedagogies and metamodelings of knowledge in the making. *CriSTaL: Critical Studies in Teaching & Learning*, 8, 1–16. DOI: 10.14426/cristal.v8iSI.261.

Nordstrom, S.N., Andersen, C.E., Osgood, J., Lorvik-Waterhouse, A.H., Otterstad, A.M., & Jensen, M. (2018). *Alice's adventures*: Reconfiguring solidarity in early childhood education and care through data events. In D. Cole & J. Bradley (Eds.), *Principles of Transversality in Globalization and Education*. Singapore: Springer. https://doi.org/10.1007/978-981-13-0583-2_11.

Osgood, J. (2008). Negotiating a professional identity in early childhood education. London Metropolitan University, PhD Thesis.

Osgood, J. (2019). Materialised reconfigurations of gender in early childhood: Playing seriously with Lego. In J. Osgood & K. Robinson (Eds.), *Feminists Researching Gendered Childhoods*, Feminist Thought in Childhood Research Series (pp. 85–108). London: Bloomsbury. Chapter 5.

Osgood, J. (2020). Becoming a 'mutated modest witness' in early childhood research. In C. Shulte (Ed.), *Ethics and Research with Young Children: New Perspectives* (pp. 113–27). London: Bloomsbury.

Osgood, J. (2022). From multispecies tangles and Anthropocene muddles: What can lichen teach us about the precarity in early childhood education? In C. Blyth & T. K. Aslanian (Eds.), *Children & the Power of Stories: Posthuman and Autoethnographic Perspectives in Early Childhood Education*. Springer.

Osgood, J., Albon, D., Allen, K., Hollingworth, S. (2012) *Engaging 'Hard to Reach' Families in Early Years Music-Making*. London: Youth Music.

Osgood, J., Albon, D., Allen, K., & Hollingworth, S. (2013). 'Hard to reach' or nomadic resistance? families 'Choosing' not to participate in early childhood services. *Global Studies of Childhood*, 3(3), 208–20. https://doi.org/10.2304/gsch.2013.3.3.208.

Osgood, J., Andersen, C. E. & Otterstad, A. M. (2022). Portal-time and wanderlines: What does virusing-with make possible in childhood research? *Reconceptualizing Educational Research Methodology*.

Rhedding-Jones, J. (2005). *What Is Research? Methodological Practices and New Approaches*. Oslo: Universiteforgalet.

Roy, A. (2022). *Azadi: Fascism, Fiction & Freedom in the Time of the Virus*. London: Penguin.

Skeggs, B. (2003). *Class, Self, Culture*. London: Routledge.

Stewart, K. (2007). *Ordinary Affects*. Durham: Duke University Press.

Stewart, K. (2011). Atmospheric attunements. *Environment and Planning D: Society & Space*, 29, 445–53.

Tsing, A. L. (2015). *The Mushroom at the End of the World: On the Possibility of Life in Capitalist Ruins*. Oxford: Princeton University Press.

Tsing, A. L., Swanson, H., Gan, E., & Bubandt, N. (Eds.) (2017). *Arts of Living on a Damaged Planet*. London: University of Minnesota Press.

4

Being there: Observing care through doing nothing in a toddler classroom

Teresa K. Aslanian
University of South-Eastern Norway

Introduction

This chapter approaches observation through Heidegger's (1962) concept of Dasein, focusing on the immersive and, I argue, intra-active relationship between humans and 'equipment'. I use experiences of failure to record observations of care beyond the human dyad in an early childhood classroom for toddlers to explore the potentially generative process of doing nothing during observations. By doing nothing, I mean choosing to stop looking for what I was looking for. In doing nothing, I became aware of 'what was happening' in a different way, through disturbances in the environment. I utilize Barad's (2014) concept of re-turning as a method to recycle, return to and re-turn Heidegger's 'Dasein' and the compulsion to return and rely on traditional data collection tools to conduct un-traditional research. This chapter generates new ways of understanding the use of traditional data collection tools to conduct un-traditional research and speculates as to alternative ways to collect and understand 'data'.

Martin Heidegger's thinking defined the early twentieth century with his disavowal of the long-accepted Cartesian idea of the isolated individual whose existence is predicated on their experience of thinking, alone. Though rarely cited in 'post' research, Heidegger's refusal of Cartesian dualism, descriptions of humans and their worlds, humans as defined through their relationship with equipment, and of care as the 'being of being', pre-dates and underlies important theoretical contributions to posthuman and feminist new materialist thought (for example Barad's (2007) intra-action, Haraway's (2016) worlding and Puig de la Bellacasa's (2012) idea of care as ontological). These scholars have extended Heidegger's thinking, but I suggest there is far more to Heidegger than has been utilized, and something to be gained by returning to and re-turning the impetus of post-thinking. Through re-turning Heidegger's conceptualization of humans and equipment, I hope to enrich and expand conceptualizations of observation as a post-qualitative research method.

The chapter is divided into two parts. First, I introduce my methodological tools that include Malabou's plasticity, Barad's re-turning and Haraway's sympoiesis. After introducing the methodological concepts, I briefly present Heidegger's (1962) Dasein as I understand it in the context of this study, and in particular Heidegger's account of the human relationship with equipment. The second part begins with a presentation of a narrative account of my failure to observe care beyond the human dyad and an analysis of how I understand the experience through Heidegger's 'being there' and a discussion of what I found in the process: academic panopticons and doing nothing as a generative force.

Methodological approach: Recycling as method

During my PhD field studies that I return to in this chapter, I sought to explore care as it materializes beyond human dyadic relations. Because I was not in the habit of seeing care in this way, I didn't know how to look for it. To observe what I didn't yet see, I looked to Wolff's (1976) method of 'catch' which he likens to love – being open to everything and using what one catches to engage with. While Wolff helped me to understand the way I 'found' data in 2016, I want to dwell longer with that experience, acknowledging that any moment entails endless scale of matters (Barad, 2014) that can be engaged with. Taking this seriously, I want to use less, and do less, in an effort to understand differently. In my earlier work, I 'recycled' Piaget's lesser-known works through Barad's concept of agential realism to explore what the two thinkers produce together and how new aspects of Piaget's thought are generated when read through Barad (Aslanian, 2017). I return to the recycling concept in this article to explore how

Heidegger's thinking can seed new ways of approaching observing more-than-human issues and processes.

Informed by Malabou's (2010, 2011) plasticity, Barad's (2017) re-turning and Haraway's (2016) sympoiesis, the idea of recycling involves engaging with potential, time and the inherent plasticity of materials and ideas. The concept of recycling has guided both how I've worked with the materials in this study and the principles that have guided it. Qualitative inquiry involves the assumption that there are no final answers to be found in qualitative work, and that analyses performed will differ according to who performs them, when and under what circumstances. But where *are* all these alternate possibilities? Malabou's plastic reading involves poking and prodding at the dormant possibilities by asking new questions of old materials or asking new questions of overlooked material (Malabou, 2011). Recycling research makes use of valuable matters, in similar or entirely new forms. Recycling nods to the awareness that there is to be found in each matter traces of many other matters, and matter, that remain unutilized until moved by some other matter to become something *both old and new*. Malabou likens it to waking 'a sleeping animal' that represents untapped potential and possibility. My hope is that through recycling 'old' data with other theories and with a new aim, the possibilities dormant in the complex materials might generate new perspectives.

Barad (2018) likens the act of re-turning to how an earthworm works its way through layers of soil, both ingesting and excreting, opening up spaces for oxygen to come in and initiate the production of new materials to ingest, excrete and burrow through, each time bringing new nutrients and burrowing new paths. I am not only re-turning however. I want to *recycle* and create something new. Heidegger (2011) conceptualizes poiesis as a *human* act of bringing forth (*with* world), bringing out something that was concealed. Haraway (2016) makes explicit that worlds are always brought forth 'together', offering the term 'sympoiesis'. While Heidegger's conception of bringing forth is a human activity and seems to allude to bringing forth something that already is, but is concealed, Haraway does not differentiate between human and more than pointing to the common creation of (non-delineated) worlds that are not being revealed, but are being re-generated in new diffractive ways. Haraway (2016) calls herself a *compostist*, stressing the common and processual role all matter on earth serves as being products of and simply part of, earth. In keeping with this thinking, I recycle my data with new theory in hopes of generating new thinking regarding postdevelopmental observation in early childhood education, and post-qualitative research.

Being in the world as 'being there', with things

Heidegger's rebuttal of Cartesian dualism at the start of the twentieth century and subject-object relations offers a curious mix of humanism and posthumansim. In this section, I present some aspects of Heidegger's thinking based mainly on his work Being and Time and various interpretations of this work, most prominently that of Dreyfuss (2007), both written and through his 2007 lecture series.

My interest in Heidegger (1962) revolves around his concept of Dasein, or 'being there'. Dasein insists on two main features: an internal relationship between a human being and their 'world' and 'taking issue' on the matter of what it is *to be*. Heidegger divides 'world' into three *modes* or *'ways of being in the world'*: substances which have properties (e.g., wood, plastic, water), objects that are used called equipment (hammers, jars, books) and Dasein (human being). It is through using equipment that humans take issue with what it is *to be*. In this way, humans' understanding of themselves is always and only gained through being already with the world. Due to this immersion, humans cannot see their world outside of their own point of view as a human in that world, because they are absorbed in it. As 'worlds', nothing is intelligible except in connection with a web of relations. Furthermore, humans do not exist in and of themselves, but only insofar as they are a part of a particular context, or web of relations. In summary, for Heidegger, being human is being absorbed in the world of things (substances and/or equipment), and to take a stand on what it is to be, through things.

Heidegger's thinking underlies post-modern thinking. Haraway and Barad build on Heidegger, extending his work with *worldhood* (Haraway, 2016) as worlding, and his division into three modes of being that only exist through each other as the beginnings of a relational ontology (Barad, 2007) through extending his thought beyond human exceptionalism. Other living beings are curiously excluded from this list and the placement of animals in this model remains under discussion. Heidegger did not believe (other) animals took a stand as to their existence, or that being was 'an issue' for them, thus, Heidegger's Dasein is exclusively human. Despite this limitation, I hope the reader will agree that the division of world into oscillating modes offers a fruitful way to understand researchers and the practice field as a multi-modal and oscillating 'world'.

The etymology of 'observe' in light of Dasein is interesting. The word 'observe' is made up of: ob 'in front of, before'. If modes oscillate according to how a thing is looked at or the condition of the thing or human, then the idea that humans direct attention to what concerns them (Heidegger, 1927/2011, p. 144 in Horrigan-Kelly et al., 2016, p. 3), could mean that we are unable to see what we are interested in seeing since in focusing on something, one sees things differently. Additionally, visual observation can never reveal aspects that are only perceptible from an ontological perspective (Dreyfus & Wrathall, 2007, p. 3). Considering the idea of human immersion in the world of equipment, an important question arises concerning observation as method: *How can we observe a world we cannot see?*

Equipment and equipment failure

The immersion of humans in their environments and the invisibility of the world of equipment within which humans are immersed present a curious foundation for approaching observation as research method. Heidegger draws our attention to the 'withdrawn-ness' of equipment when it is in use or when it functions as 'ready-to-hand'. His classic example is of a hammer that, while we are hammering is invisible for us, we see only the nail going in. When equipment does not function however, the invisibility of it as something *used* (ready-at-hand) turns into something *present* (present-at-hand), a presence that does not go away and that, somehow, brings the context of which it was a part to light that previously was hidden in the action of it being used. Entities oscillate between being present-at-hand or ready-at-hand (Glendinning, 1998), at least from the perspective of Dasein. Humans use equipment to 'cope' with existence. While equipment functions, and we, through equipment, cope, the equipment is invisible for us. Furthermore, it is through equipment that we function as parent, teacher, lawyer. A person uses equipment to do and be what they are. For example, my computer and my books are what make me a researcher.

Equipment in use is 'ready-at-hand' *until* something comes along that disturbs the 'coping'. A changed perspective on something, staring at the hammer until its form is more prominent than its function, or the hammer somehow becomes deformed and no longer can function, creates a disturbance. Disturbances bring to the fore the characteristic of *present-at-hand* in what is *ready-at-hand*. Present-at-hand means that equipment becomes a thing, a substance. It gains a conspicuous un-usability. When a thing loses its 'assignment', its assignment becomes explicit. The non-hammering hammering of a hammer that cannot hammer appears for us explicitly, while the hammering of a hammer hammering retreats into the background. A sewing machine that cannot sew almost screams about its function that it cannot perform, whereas a sewing machine that functions disappears, and our eyes see the material being sewn together. Equipment reveals its usefulness only through not being able to be used, when 'the assignment (of the thing) becomes explicit', conspicuous, obtrusive and obstinate (Heidegger, 1962, p. 103).

In the following section, I share my experience of failing to record my observations with equipment that goes from ready-at-hand to present-at-hand, when it fails to function for my research purpose.

Equipment failure and doing nothing

The subject of care in ECEC was my interest area, and inspired by Barad, I was curious as to how care materialized beyond (human) dyadic relations. My plan to explore care beyond the dyad was to observe a Norwegian ECEC centre for toddlers, over a three-week period. I planned to collect data from my observations with notetaking (pen and hand-sized notepad), and photographs (iPhone camera). During my first days observing, I held my pen and notepad in hand as I sat and watched from the couch or wandered around the rooms. I felt a sharp panic as to what was worthy of writing down in notes that would become my data. When would I 'see' care beyond the dyad? Where was it hiding? I looked. I wrote down some short descriptions of what I saw happening around me. The words seemed feeble, not capturing what I had noticed at all. I photographed objects that seemed to be related to care: the toy bed for the dolls, the mat children were playing on ... were these materializations of care? My photos did not capture the feeling of care I was experiencing. I felt a tiny but growing feeling of panic. I was looking for something that was not something yet established as existing: care beyond the human dyad in an ECEC centre. I was trying to extend my thinking, but also abide by certain well-established rules and rigour. I felt the eyes of the invisible but present research community, including my supervisors and the authors of articles I was building my research approach on like an invisible consort. After a couple days of writing hollow words in my notepad and half-heartedly taking photos on my iPhone of things that I deemed part of care processes I was observing, I gave up on my notepad and iPhone and put them down, sat myself down on the couch and did nothing.

Slowly, impressions of my original intention for the study began to arise in my thoughts and even my body. In the presence of this awareness of my intention for the study, my own presence, standing in the classroom with impotent tools became very strange to me. As I became strange to myself, the sounds of the classroom were at once more prominent and stranger as well. Impressions from things around me announced themselves as both impersonal, persistent, and present. Somehow, the environment announced itself to me differently when I stopped trying to see and record. In the days that followed, I did not try to see or find care, and instead tried to just be there. After some days of nothing, certain sounds and smells stood out from the background nothingness: a preschool teacher humming, the smell of bread baking, and a crash of toys and the silence that followed. These sensory experiences became the data material I used to understand care beyond the dyad.

Re-turning the narrative with Heidegger

In this section, I explore the above narrative through Heidegger's ideas concerning Dasein and equipment. According to Heidegger, my notepad, pen and iPhone made me into a researcher. It was along with these tools that I became a researcher, connected to the traditions and knowledge of my field. We were to work together, my notepad, pen, iPhone and I, to observe and extract meaning from the situation I entered into as an observer. But what *kind* of researcher was I to be, as defined by whom? And what was the 'it' I could observe with these tools?

The academic panopticon

As a female PhD student, I had absorbed certain expectations about how to observe, and what a rigorous design entailed. It is well established, however, that preoccupation with how things should be done, with technique and protocol can hinder reflective thinking. A researcher's work is to be transparent, so that the work can be judged by peers as either legitimate or illegitimate. I must make choices and explain those choices, reflecting on how those choices affect my data and the work as a whole. I was expected to act independently, making choices during my fieldwork that I must later describe in the research article that was to be a kind of final product. The reflections and thinking that underlies my choices are informed by the work done by my predecessors in the academy. I had to do it *right*, while at the same time, my intention was to push boundaries, to let unique and unexpected thinking patterns emerge and see 'more than' I had seen previously.

Turning over these reflections with Heidegger, I am reminded of Foucault's panopticon. Foucault's (1988) interest in the panopticon as means of control and subjectification can be applied to environments beyond the prison system. As an architectural system designed to control as many inmates with as little work as possible, the panopticon's design allowed inmates in a circular design of cells to be seen by prison guards residing in the centre of the circle, through a backlighting system. In this way, the prisoners could be seen, but the prisoners could not see who was looking at them or know for sure if anyone was looking at them, they only knew that a guard *could be* looking at them at any moment (Penfield, 2017). As an early career researcher, I was acutely aware of the possibility established researchers had to accuse me of unscientific work, unethical work or simply work that was not 'theoretical' enough. With the humility and acknowledgement that my situation as a privileged, white American academic working in Norway and being paid to undertake a study that I wanted to undertake cannot be compared to the experiences of prison inmates that lived in the panopticon described here, I only mean to make a connection between the general design of panoptic control and the positioning of those who know and have the power to decide in academia and those who these decisions and appraisals are acted upon. My work was to be described and published in print and permanently on display to be judged by members of the academy who could either support me or criticize, or even discredit me. I could never know who will read my work and how it will be judged. The result is that I, like the inmates of a panopticon, internalize the judgements my senior peers could make, constraining my field of movement and imagined opportunities for thinking and acting outside of the academic norms and rules I have spent the past year internalizing. About the panopticon, Foucault writes:

> He who is subjected to a field of visibility, and who knows it, assumes responsibility for the constraints of power; he makes them play spontaneously upon himself; he inscribes in himself the power relation in which he simultaneously plays both roles; he becomes the principle of his own subjection.
>
> (Foucault, 1995, p. 195)

My predecessors, supervisors and future colleagues based their choices on the work of their predecessors, supervisors and future colleagues. For me, predecessors included both men and women, while for some of my predecessors, this included only men. The traditions dictating what made research legitimate were not only prescribed by men, but also by men in relation to studies with goals and concerned with issues relating to anthropocentric and to a certain degree, positivistic traditions.

Returning to the narrative, when my equipment failed, my self-doubt came to light in a new way, and I became aware of ideas that were not my own, policing my research behaviour. The panopticon compels us to see only that which others see, that has already been regarded as 'real'. Penfield (2017) describes the inmates of a panopticon as being ceaselessly subject to the certain possibility (though uncertain reality) of being observed, the inmate internalizes the panoptic gaze by incorporating its normalizing judgement as the rule guiding and constraining his or her own conduct (Penfield, 2017). Nordstrom (2017, p. 221) describes her struggle to research more-than-human worlds within the systemic demands for traditional research methods:

> I have to position the methodology and methods of data collection as static entities. I have to anticipate all the data I will collect and all the ethical issues that might arise during the study. I have to anticipate how participants might respond to interview questions and any possible discomfort and gains from participating in the study. Simply put, I have to both discursively and materially produce a study within positivism so that it will be sanctioned by those in power.

Nordstrom (2017) responds by thinking with Deleuze and Guattari's concept of 'and' as ground of becoming, to resist the idea of researching distinct objects that already are. My approach stems from the same issue but finds the solution in not only thinking differently, but also doing something differently – stopping with my whole body and doing nothing until something happens that is not expected and could not be foreseen, that propels me into a new position. This way, my action is propelled by 'being there' rather than the panopticon of expectations and tradition of what the field *is*, and what researching *is*.

Doing nothing

Nothingness is often conceptualized as a void or emptiness (Barad, 2018). In other words, it is conceptualized as a place – or as a place that is not. Heidegger points to 'nothing' as manifest in Dasein and key to accessing and being overwhelmed by 'the total strangeness of beings' that evokes wonder and the impulse to ask 'why?' (Heidegger, 2011).

Nothing, or the void, is not only a conceptual state of non-being, but also (potentially) something that can be 'done', perhaps as an act of oxymoroning

(Reinersten, 2021), *doing* nothing. How do we do nothing? What are we doing when we do nothing? St. Pierre (2011, p. 623) asks, 'what might happen if we give up exhausted structures and [instead] attend to what is happening'? How do we 'attend to what is happening'? How do we see when how we think affects what we *can* see? Can 'doing nothing' be a start? Following Heidegger, being eludes both observation and contemplation. There is then something in everything that exceeds what we can behold, access or describe. Nothing can therefore ever be fully disclosed by how it appears (Harman, 2010).

I did nothing by resisting the urge to do something. I sat on the couch and was just being there. Perhaps something close to a meditative state was reached when certain sounds and other sensory perceptions impressed themselves upon me. First a teacher humming, then the smell of bread, and then some plastic toys crashing on the floor and an ensuing silence. These sensorial impressions were disruptions to the nothing I was doing. In the tradition of Dada and rebellious movements from time immemorial, disturbing the status quo provokes change. Anything that happens, happens because something moves something else in a way that provokes a change in course. It is disturbance that instigates a new perspective on that which is usually unseen and out-of-view.

Nordstrom et al. (2018) created disturbances to subvert expectations of academic conferencing and concepts of solidarity that produced complex results, with audience members/participants not always wanting to be disturbed. I suggest disturbances do not need to be created, but researchers can choose to make themselves receptive to being disturbed, by doing nothing. Disturbances occur continuously. Being receptive to disturbances requires a rethinking of a research plan and the idea of responsibility, where the plan involves a starting point relating to the researchers' goal, who stays interested and alert to what disturbances can disclose about the situation at hand. Being disturbed while doing nothing is experiencing something different that announces its presence through giving substance to an otherwise invisible world. In words, it might look something like this:

nothing
nothing
nothing
nothing
something

nothing
nothing
something

Ehn and Löfgren (2010) studied what people do when they 'do nothing', and describe how data observations appeared out of nowhere, while they were on the move and their minds were drifting. Phenomena that otherwise seemed like 'nothing' when doing 'something', became 'something' when doing 'nothing'; the smell of bread baking, the sound of a teacher humming, the crash of plastic toys, silence.

Post-qualitative research is concerned with subject matters and has intentions that diverge from the concerns and aims of methodologies underlying traditional methods that we continue to rely on (Nordstrom, 2017). St. Pierre (2019) suggests traditional methods are incompatible with post-qualitative research. Ultimately, I found the photos I took of the things that most corresponded to my sensorial experiences of care beyond the dyad were more useful to think with than my written notes. However, it was my memory of the sensations, the sounds and the totality of my expectations being subverted somehow by happenings in the environment that provided me with data to think with. The photos aided my ability to tell the story of my observations, my participation in the classroom and my search for care in the environment, but they by no means 'captured' care in the classroom.

My memories of impressions from observation generate connections between the handwritten notes, photographs, smells, sounds and ideas about home, care, ECEC and children, myself as a researcher, the Nordic kindergarten tradition, capitalism, social democracy, international competitiveness, developmental psychology and more. Memories weigh heavier on a particular sense, sight, smell, hearing, touch – but then spread to other nerves of thought and memory, providing a rich tapestry for thinking about care beyond the dyad in ECEC toddler classroom, far richer than my iPhone and notepad alone are able to record. Through doing nothing, therefore, I was able to receive impressions I may not have been sensitive to had I been actively looking for care and that enriched the traditional data supplied by notetaking and photographing what I could see. I was able to experience the field in a way that provided a generative representation of my experiences of *being there, being disturbed* and experiencing *care*. Care is something we are *doing* in our world, since we are immersed in the world of equipment, which is a doing, not a thing-ing. We observe to gain insight into things that happen during more-than-human processes. Doing nothing and allowing oneself to be disturbed may be a mode of accessing the unknown or unknowable. New insight might be gained by a breaking down or malfunctioning of tools, or a change in human relating to the tools that renders tools no longer useful and thus suddenly present-at-hand. This underlines an intra-dependence between what Heidegger describes as humans, substances and equipment.

Though my equipment didn't function in the way I had assumed it would or planned it to, it did *do* something. The photographs aided my thinking and triggered memories and connections between memories. The notes reminded me of how I perceived the field at the time of writing them – representing my uncertainty more than what the words on the notepad were pointing to. They also help to re-animate the experience of writing hollow words about things and people out of context – and the act of writing the words, acting within a panopticon, unauthentic and moving against my own better judgement and knowledge. The notes are evidence of a complexity of researching and observing in the 'field'. Photographs and notes helped me construct an analysis of my memory data and material data together.

Something old and new

In this article, I've tried to recycle Heidegger's ideas through re-turning data to explore 'being there' as a way to collect data and learn about more-than-human processes. I wanted to bring something new forth from something old through composting, returning philosophical thinking and dwelling longer with old data. Recycling philosophy, data and narrative experience as sympoiesis (Haraway, 2016) does not produce answers, but can hopefully generate more thought that transcends ideas of 'old' and 'new'.

Foucault (1988) commented in his final interview that he uses Heidegger as an 'instrument of thought'. In embracing the thinking of a problematic thinker, this article has brought along with it pain from the past, Heidegger's flirtation with Nazism, and his analytical blind spot regarding the lives of other-than-human animals. Recycling as a process of research embraces re-turning, but also insists on a generative outcome, that punctuates a continual process of re-turning. Returning without re-turning is not necessarily a generative strategy. As a PhD student for example, I unconsciously returned to traditional modes of collecting data, without reflecting on the ontological basis of traditional observation methods, and found myself within an academic panopticon. This article has addressed challenges researchers face when observing more-than-human processes through Heidegger's account of humans and equipment. The cryptic oscillation between different modes of being in the world as 'present at hand' and 'ready at hand', and the potentially generative activity of doing nothing and *being there* can perhaps offer a 'way out' of the academic panopticon for post-qualitative researchers.

References

Aslanian, T. K. (2017). Recycling Piaget: Posthumanism and making children's knowledge matter. *Educational Philosophy & Theory*. http://dx.doi.org/10.1080/00131857.2017.1377068.

Barad, K. (2007). *Meeting the Universe Halfway: Quantum Physics and the Entaglement of Matter and Meaning*. Durham: Duke University Press.

Barad, K. (2014). Diffracting diffraction: Cutting together-apart. *Parallax, 20*(3), 168–87. https://doi.org/10.1080/13534645.2014.927623.

Barad, K. (2018). Troubling time/s and ecologies of nothingness: Re-turning, re-membering, and facing the incaculable. In M. Fritsch, P. Lynes, & D. Wood (Eds.), *Eco-Deconstruction: Derrida and Environmental Philosophy* (Vol. 92, pp. 56–86). Fordham University Press. https://doi.org/https://doi.org/10.3898/NEWF:92.05.2017.

de la Bellacasa, M. P. (2012). 'Nothing comes without its world': Thinking with care. *The Sociological Review, 60*(2), 197–216. https://doi.org/10.1111/j.1467-954X.2012.02070.x.

Dreyfus, H. L., & Wrathall, M. A. (2007). *A Companion to Heidegger*. John Wiley & Sons, Incorporated.

Ehn, B. & Löfgren, O. (2010). *The Secret World of Doing Nothing*. Oakland: University of California Press.

Farell Krell, D. (Ed.) (2011/1977). *Heidegger. Basic Writings*. London: Routledge.

Foucault, M. (1988). *Michel Foucault. Politics Philosophy Culture.* Interviews and other writings 1977-1984 (A. Sheridan, Trans.; L. D. Kritszman, Ed.). London: Routledge.

Foucault, M. (1995). *Discipline & Punish: The Birth of the Prison* (2nd ed.). London: Vintage.

Glendinning, S. (1998). *On Being with Others: Heidegger, Wittgenstein, Derrida.* London: Taylor & Francis Group.

Haraway, D. (2016). *Staying with the Trouble: Making Kin in the Chthulucene.* Durham: Duke University.

Harman, G. (2010). Technology, objects and things in heidegger. *Cambridge Journal of Economics, 34*(1), 17–25. http://www.jstor.org/stable/24232017.

Heidegger, M. (1962). *Being and Time* (J. Macquarrie & E. Robinson, Trans.). New York: Harper & Row.

Heidegger, M. (2011). *Martin Heidegger.* Basic Writings. (D. F. Krell, Ed.). London: Routledge.

Horrigan-Kelly, M., Millar, M., & Dowling, M. (2016). Understanding the key tenets of Heidegger's philosophy for interpretive phenomenological research. *International Journal of Qualitative Methods, 15*(1). https://doi.org/10.1177/1609406916680634.

Malabou, C. (2010). *Plasticity at the Dusk of Writing: Dialectic, Destruction, Deconstruction.* New York: Columbia University Press.

Malabou, C. (2011). Like a Sleeping Animal – philosophy between presence and absence. *Inaesthetics 2, Animailty.*

Murris, K. (Ed.) (2021). *A Glossary for Doing Postqualitative, New Materialist and Critical Posthumanist Research across Disciplines* (1st ed.). London: Routledge. https://doi.org/https://doi.org/10.4324/9781003041153.

Nordstrom, S. N. (2017). Antimethodology: Postqualitative generative conventions. *Qualitative Inquiry, 24*(3), 215–26. https://doi.org/10.1177/1077800417704469.

Nordstrom, S. N., Andersen, C. E., Osgood, J., Lorvik-Waterhouse, A.-H., Otterstad, A. M., & Jensen, M. (2018). Alice's adventures: Reconfiguring solidarity in early childhood education and care through data events. In D. R. Cole & J. P. N. Bradley (Eds.), *Principles of Transversality in Globalization and Education* (pp. 175–93). Springer Singapore. https://doi.org/10.1007/978-981-13-0583-2_11.

Penfield, C. (2017). Carceral, Capital, Power: The 'Dark Side' of the Enlightenment in Discipline and Punish in Understanding Foucault, Understanding Modernism, edited by David Scott, Bloomsbury Academic & Professional, 2017. ProQuest Ebook Central, http://ebookcentral.proquest.com/lib/ucsn-ebooks/detail.action?docID=4773174.

Puig de la Bellacasa, M. (2012). 'Nothing comes without its world': Thinking with care. *The Sociological Review, 60*(2), 197–216. https://doi.org/10.1111/j.1467-954X.2012.02070.x.

Reinertsen, A. B. (2021). The art of not knowing, the position of non-knowledge as activisms. *International Review of Qualitative Research.* ISSN 1940-8447. *14*(3), 476–82. DOI: 10.1177/1940844720948067.

Sheehan, T. (2007). Dasein. In H. L. Dreyfus & M. A. Wrathall (Eds.), *A Companion to Heidegger* (pp. 193–213). New Jersey: John Wiley & Sons, Incorporated.

St. Pierre, E. A. (2011). Post qualitative research: The critique and the coming after. In N. K. Denzin & Y. S. Lincoln (Eds.), *The SAGE Handbook of Qualitative Research* (pp. 611–26). London: Sage.

St. Pierre, E. A. (2019). Post qualitative inquiry, the refusal of method, and the risk of the new. *Qualitative Inquiry, 27*(1), 3–9. https://doi.org/10.1177/1077800419863005.

Thoibisana, A. (2008). Heidegger on the notion of dasein as habited body. *Indo-Pacific Journal of Phenomenology, 8*(2), 1–5. https://doi.org/10.1080/20797222.2008.11433968.

Wolff, K. (1976). *Surrender and Catch: Experience and Inquiry Today.* New York: Springer.

Telling story: The Carrier Bag theory of Fiction as a means of reciprocal 'researching-with' children

Victoria de Rijke
Middlesex University

Introduction to reciprocal practice

This chapter will explore the (idealistic but not utopian) idea of reciprocal arts education practice as a means of 'researching-with' children. From the etymology of *reciprocus* (based on *re-* 'back' + *pro-* 'forward'), it will move backward and forward in time as a reciprocal method arguing for postdevelopmental, agential observations in practice research, looking closely and critically at the author's experiences of working collaboratively with children, proposing creative method and artwork *as* 'ontological relationality' (Braidotti, 2013) and research outcome.

This chapter owes a debt to the encouragement and support of colleague Jayne Osgood, who, with Red Ruby Scarlet and Miriam Giugni (2015) argued the case for posthumanist research to be seen as 'theory and method and art'. Reflecting on experimental, arts-based inquiry, concerned with how 'the vitality of matter, affect, discourse, bodies (human and non-human) and place "intra-act" in assemblages … for what might be questioned, shared, politicized and transformed', they seek not to pose solutions or conclusions but 'rather to create a space to encourage halting conversations about gender that transmute and reconstitute irreducible details along lines of continuation, interruption and reformulation' (Osgood et al., 2015, p. 357). I will argue that forms of this Baradian 'response-ability' can be enacted by storying through socially engaged arts practices of dialogue, photography and education resource-making.

In the pocket-size essay *The Carrier Bag Theory of Fiction* (2019), writer Ursula Le Guin uses the analogy of early humans sloping off to hunt mammoths to form the quintessential (patriarchal) tale of heroism, since: 'it wasn't the meat that made the difference. It was the story' (1996, p. 149). Her feminist reworking suggests a collective, inclusive reconsideration of fiction, narrative and heroism; namely some kind of container to 'bring energy home'. As she describes, a container is needed if one does not want to miss anything and to carry, collect and store food, meat, oats, fruit, berries, seed and children: 'A leaf a gourd a shell a net a bag a sling a sack a bottle a pot a box a container. A holder. A recipient' (Le Guin, 1996, p. 150).

Teachers as borderline artist/cultural workers

My education arts practice began with my first job in a Primary school (set in a 'social priority' area of north London) in the 1980s. I quickly felt a sense of growing unease with the limits placed on children by their apparent different 'ability', plus further weights of difference/othering based on privilege/class/race/gender and so on, and the generally anti-democratic nature of teaching itself, even pre-National Curriculum. As a child of European migrants to the UK, I found the metaphor of 'borderline artists' and 'dangerous border crossers' liberating for my sense of identity and practice. Giroux described such artists as:

> cultural workers whose public function offers them the opportunity to serve as border intellectuals who engage in a productive dialogue across different sites of cultural production. [...] At stake here is not merely the opportunity to link art to practices that are transgressive and oppositional, but also to make visible a wider project of connecting forms of cultural production to the creation of multiple critical public spheres.
>
> (Giroux, 1995, p. 5)

It was exhilarating as a newly qualified teacher to view myself a cultural worker/borderline artist educator, pursuing interdisciplinary inquiry, aiming to up-end established hierarchies between artist and audience, expert and novice, for new forms of community and participation; what Freire (2001) called 'transformative education' for change. *Toys: Are they Playing with You?* was a photographic project instigated after asking the class what they wanted to be when they grew up, when, to my dismay, many responses and aspirations seemed drastically regulated by gender. Using toys as a metaphor for sociocultural gender stereotyping, we discussed which toys might be aimed and marketed at girls or boys, the toys they played with and why, what new gender-free toys they could invent and what their carers thought of toys and gender. We drew, photographed and collaged as we went along. To separate this project from daily lessons, the method was deliberately intuitive, looking for the unexpected, listening to children and developing activities based on their emerging agenda, rather than pre-planned teaching. This research into the effect of toys on gender stereotyping culminated in a touring exhibition: *Toys: Are They Playing with You?* (with Cockpit Gallery), which to our collective pride became a Fawcett Society Award Winner (1987). The Fawcett Society persists with award-winning campaigns like *Let Toys Be Toys* (2022).

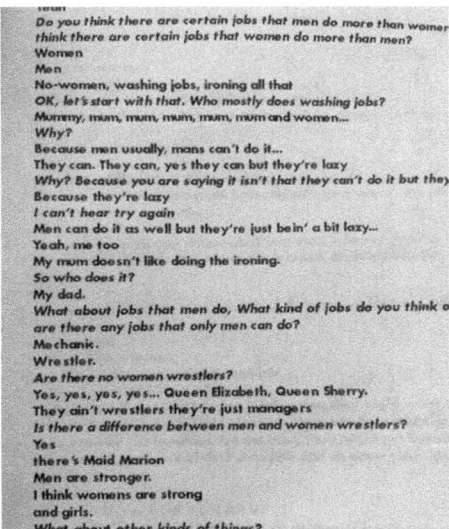

Figure 5.1 Transcript excerpt of class conversation.

Figure 5.2 Poster for exhibition at Cockpit Gallery 1987.

Collage/assemblage

I was naturally drawn to the technique of collage when working with children, because the process allows for a hybrid assemblage of what children saw as 'grown-up', 'finished' or 'more real' photographic images (like those cut out from newspapers and magazines) juxtaposed with their own sketching, drawing and writing (which they often described as 'messy', 'not real enough', etc.). Collage was thus an amalgamation of adult and child-led arts practices. In what was already an age of image saturation, photography was also an accessible medium through which to question stereotype, truth, bias, motive, and was part of an arts momentum in 'progressive', socially engaged, community education arts practice. In 1986, Bezencenet argued that: 'if we consider education to be a process of acquiring and investigating knowledge in order to achieve a competence and pleasure in critically understanding social differences, then photography can have a substantial role within the system' (in de Rijke, 1996, npn).

Mindful of feminist critiques about the risks of voyeurism and what Berger termed the 'male gaze' (1972) inherent in much photographic practice, we used a cable-release technique to mitigate risks of unequal agency. The camera is jointly set up on a tripod by adult and child, and a long cable is run from shutter to sitter, so that each child decides independently when and how to take their picture. As the cable-release device itself was a source of fascination and often featured in children's drawings, the autonomy of clicking the shutter themselves was evidently important. Who takes the picture and how it gets taken matters.

The cable release method curiously offers what might be understood as posthuman ontological relationality. A relational, enlarged sense of connection between self and others (by removing the self-centred individualism of the 'self-portrait') can be achieved by this method. For the desired expression, children had to consult with collaborators assisting with the process, take on advice and encouragement, but ultimately choose the decisive moment for their own image. In the collages below, five- and six-year-old children took their own portraits which I printed, gave back to them to cut out and assemble

Figure 5.3 L-R drawing the cable release in action.

Figure 5.4 By Yelda. Girls' collages for career choices often included those they would be 'helping' (pupils, animals, etc.) whereas.

Figure 5.5 By Ka is an example of how boys more often depicted themselves as authoritative.

into collages of their career aspirations. The children's facial expressions are therefore those of the jobs they are enacting: in this case, firm but fair.

Arts practices like collage allow for diverse contribution that acknowledges and is adaptive to difference (Bjerke's idea of 'differently equal' 2011, such as variable pace, children dictate orally, adult writes/records; children and adults discuss design decisions voted on democratically). Fairness and honesty create conditions of mutual trust and respect. Project topics familiar to children that stem from childhood cultural experience about which they can be expert (cf. Coyne & Carter's reminder that children are 'expert in their own lives' rather than unreliable informants of those lives (2018, p. 3) also allow for *matter* that *matters:* time is given to investigate concrete object relations and materialities.

In a recent article written collaboratively with two adults and a child, the authors stated that

> the child of the Anthropocene is not fully formed: it is a child waiting to become fully human once it has passed through ages and stages that are closely monitored and measured against normative expectations. Conceptualisations of the child are shaped by futurity; who and what the child will become; the ultimate goal is to become adult.
> (de Rijke, Osgood & Williams, 2023, p. 155)

Questioning children seriously about what they want to be (and why) when they grow up and role-play is thus as important for children as adults when researching and challenging what 'futurity' might mean, *or be limited to.*

Feminist scholarship (e.g. Hughes & Lury, 2013; Renold & Mellor, 2013), in highlighting the omnipresence of dominant systems of power (class, race, gender, age and so on), reveals decades of persistent concern with positionality, relationality and interdisciplinarity, with what can be known and who can be a knower, and with the centrality of ethical, transformative practices within relations of power, asking: 'What counts as valid knowledge? Who decides? Who consents? Why? and on what grounds?' (Lather, 1993). This questioning, and responses to it, marks key shifts towards an ethical 'being-with' others and geopolitical feminist/posthumanist 'worldly' 'becoming', rather than erroneous claims of scientific objectivity (Haraway, 2008, p. 356).

Reciprocal talk

Communication is the search for meaning and understanding. Open, participatory conversation allows room for experiential knowledge and 'figurative thought' often regarded as 'childish' (Jenks, 2005). Talk is part of knowledge production, which can be inventive or humorous response discussions (e.g. Benton & Fox, 1985), where play is a language force and decolonizing strategy (e.g. Brice-Heath, 2009), and talk performs creative reasoning.

Kester (1999) explored the role of conversation and dialogue in arts practice as 'socially engaged art', which connected strongly with my own (lasting) educational belief that literacy is founded on oracy (rather than prioritizing reading or writing, which can de-skill children). Kester describes specific examples where conversation is 'reframed as an active, generative process that can help us speak and imagine beyond the limits of fixed identities and official discourse' (1999, p. 78). I imagined I could position my classroom as an 'intersection of education, art and activism': a 'relational site for meaningful border crossing and productive dialogue that could re-imagine larger social expectations for art and education' (Hamlyn, 2017), and that valuing talk and visual literacy were key components to go in the bag.

Haraway's introduction to Le Guin's carrier-bag theory of fiction suggests that 'bag lady story telling' or researching with 'unexpected partners' is like throwing ideas into a 'frayed, porous carrier bag' (Haraway, 2004, p. 127). I was beginning to believe that the porous and changing boundaries of child and adult arts education research – engaging in (similarly porous) dialogic conversation – could work towards disassembling structural inequalities and normative or oppressive power relations, for new creative knowledges.

In this way, children's views are taken seriously. They are treated as equal knowers and artists. Equally, participatory research *requires* the adult to become a co-learner (cf. Coyne & Carter, 2018) with benefits of following threads of children's devising. Projects that foreground oracy (e.g. reciprocal talk, questioning, conversation, discussion, debate, interview) as knowledge exchange (rather than written literacy), position learning as 'thinking with' arts practice. Visual arts making (e.g. drawing, photography, collage, objects) is valued as haptic knowledge production, where *how* we are making is the knowledge product. If adults make alongside children, their role is also maker, not observer, and the art is shared, active, discursive, creative and process-driven (laying bare the device).

Supertoys

In this optimistic spirit I revisited toys again twenty years later with the *Supertoy* project, working as part of an independent artist/educator team (Kahve-Society, with Geoff Cox and Hatice Abdullah), ninety nine- and ten-year-old children from Headley Primary School in Bristol and the Arnolfoni Gallery. Inspired by Aldiss's sci-fi story *Supertoys Last All Summer Long* (1969) about a cyborg/ersatz child and robot teddy discussing what *is* real, and what love might mean (in a cold and alienated machine world), the project sought to research toys and play, but in ways that resisted developmental, normative conceptualizations. Winnicott's *Playing and Reality* (1971) explored the processes of projection and identification that imbues toys with meaning through play via object relations theory.[1] Playing *with* children allowed for a shared reality that could co-make meaning across the children's inner and outer worlds.

As commercial toys are absolutely both part of children's culture and the adult material world given to them/inflicted on them, the *Supertoy* project questioned why children are largely disenfranchised in this process, in that they play with toys, but have little input into their politics, design or production. The research began by investigating toy advertising and marketing, with children creating jingles and logos, including one for the project. (see Fig 5.6)

Our research was founded on Winnicott's object relations theory and Klein's notion of the 'perfect object which is in pieces' (1935). Klein had recognized the rage of the child who first sees a 'loved object' or carer as 'perfect', then tries to make reparation for flawed care to restore the 'good object' (or 'good enough' parenting, as Winnicott put it). (Rage against) Toys can act as transference objects for this therapeutic process.

Our project's satiric method was more like the malevolent child character 'Sid' in Pixar's animation *Toy Story* (1995), as children and adults broke up

Figure 5.6 *Supertoy* logo designed by children, featuring the hybrid toy 'Captain Bear Beak'.

old toys and inventively recycled or rebuilt them into hybrids. Because of the relational psychological significance of this, we made clear distinctions in the project between beloved toys (invariably teddies, dolls and cuddly animals) that were brought in for their owners to tell stories about and not damaged, versus those that were no longer in use, so could be broken up and re-constituted. As Winnicott's theory was that an object must be capable of withstanding both destructive and loving impulses in order to become real, the project inquired deeply into what made play 'real', working towards children examining play and designing toys for themselves that resisted gender or childist stereotype.

The children's work formed the starting point and a substantial part of an exhibition *Supertoys: Play, Affective Machines and Object Relations* held at the Arnolfini Gallery, Bristol in 2008. A 'toy factory' was installed in the gallery for visitors to destroy donated unwanted toys and reassemble new ones which were then displayed on shelving. Highly original for exhibiting children's work on an equal basis as the adult artwork, and hugely popular with public of all ages, the exhibition period had children managing adult public engagement making new supertoys in the gallery. In this way, adults and children played

Figure 5.7 Some 'mutant' toy examples made by children from Headley Primary School, Bristol.

Figure 5.8 Toys made by the public in the Arnolfini gallery.

Figure 5.9 Making in the gallery.

with different combinations (of toy parts) as a form of thinking-with, entering into a collaborative research practice of 'liveability, impermanence and emergence' (Tsing, 2015, p. 158). As Le Guin demonstrated in all her writing and as Tsing argues, 'assemblages coalesce, change, and dissolve; this *is* the story'.

This project had several revelatory moments: positive and negative. The first was when the adult group met the children with whom they would be working, and to quickly bond and form relationships of trust and playfulness, we played outside in the school playground with them for the first week. It was shocking how much of the play was gendered: boys playing Transformers (adaptive, armoured vehicles) war games or football, with girls sitting in groups out of harm's way brushing Barbie dolls. As part of the project, we took a trip to a local *Toys R Us* store, noting all kinds of marketing strategies (such as the blue and pink aisles and packaging for gender segregated toys) and began our conversations, children bringing in loved toys as well as discarded or broken ones. Opportunities to link their thoughts and feelings with Winnicottian object relations theory were surprisingly easy: they quickly grasped the concept, used psychoanalytic vocabulary confidently in discussion and were remarkably open about their feelings of rage, hurt, disappointment, frustration or love, tenderness and security that marked their relationships with toys.

Conversation between A(author) Curtis, Kila & Emma (age 9&10) about being 'lost in play'

A: How do you get lost in play?
E: You get lost in play because you're in the middle bit and not round the edges.
K: You get lost in play because it feels like you're in another dimension.
*C: You get lost in play because you feel like you're not playing the game anymore; you **are** the game.*

How is playing like dreaming?
E: Playing is like dreaming because you have to ask yourself: is it real or is it not?
K: Playing is like dreaming because it can be as imaginative as you want it to be.

A: Is playing controlled?

C: It's like, if you're bored, and you've got nothing to do, and your mind's just like 'bleuah' and there's nothing going on in it, and then you get like a little idea and it just pops and there's loads of little things going on in it and it just goes out of control, like something growing ...
E: Nothing going on inside your imagination, and then you like see something or hear something or remember something and then you get this little like seed of an idea and then it just explodes and you get all these different ideas to do with it, and then it's like you can't control the ideas because they just keep coming.
K: It's like when you find that toy, when you start playing with that toy, it's like it's got a soul.

In this extract, the marginal or subordinate role children often feel they occupy is transformed into an exchange between one-other that builds incrementally on their innovative imagery 'you *are* the game'; 'like something growing'; 'little like seed of an idea', very like Le Guin's irreducible pieces in the porous carrier bag. This means not shying away from risk or using complex theoretical models as anything can be made accessible to children (cf. Bruner's 1960 viewpoint that any subject can be taught effectively in some intellectually honest form to any child at any stage of development).

A further revelation was the extent to which the adults ultimately disappointed the children, by not delivering on a (shared but frankly utopian) goal that the best (by majority vote) gender-free toy design might become marketed for real (*if* we could find funding to patent it, but we couldn't). I felt this as a betrayal of a goal received as a promise, and though we got very close (3-D printing a prototype of the chosen toy design, and attempting to find interest), the adults' lack of business acumen fell short of this ambition. Empowered partly by the project experience to speak their minds, several children upbraided us angrily, which was hurtful (though fair, and testament to our relations of mutual trust – for honest exchange, at least).

Their damaged trust was somewhat alleviated by exhibiting with – but presenting *without* – adults at the Arnolfini Gallery, dominating a vast lecture space with a very strong verbal group presentation of their thoughts about gender and toys, showing their drawings, writing and toy designs, and contributing to a book: *Supertoys: A User's Manual*, which presented the project as a model for similar arts education practice. Children did sketches for the book's overall design and content such as using simple shapes 'because we don't know what toys the reader might be using' and passing on their

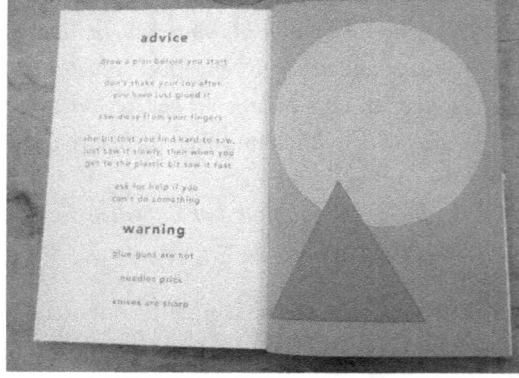

Figure 5.10 *Supertoys* manual.   **Figure 5.11** Page of advice to child readers.

experience with advice about using tools safely: 'saw away from your fingers', 'don't shake your toy after you have just glued it', 'glue guns are hot' and 'ask for help if you can't do something'.

Agential questioning

Like Dewey's idea of 'conjoint action', which sees agency as a drive leading to a notion of a 'public' that develops critical citizenship and can then take public action, political philosopher and activist Arendt examines what empowerment might be by beginning with agency. She describes it as 'acting in concert to create something new or "unexpected," for "publicness" where a multiplicity of voices and opinions creates "plurality". This plurality is a community interconnectedness she calls 'interspace', 'in between' or 'inter-est' that tolerates difference without the need to smooth it out in agreement. Children argue as bitterly over gender difference as adults do and deserve 'inter-est' safe spaces to have these disputes as part of researching their own cultures of difference. Barad argues (2007, p. 148), all research is 'an apparatus, a *doing*, not a thing', and that doing enacts 'agential cuts' (specific intra-actions and boundary-making, such as deciding 'what matters and is excluded from mattering').

As Arendt argued, Totalitarianism works to destroy the public realm and demands a single voice. But normalizing power can be resisted and transformed; empowerment is not tolerating or making allowance for difference, it is learning how to share the world by means of questioning and challenging the power/voices of dominant groups. Research into Dolci's radical education practice reminds me of the powerful threads connecting his, Arendt's and Freire's action against oppression, where education is 'the practice of freedom', and 'thinking from the standpoint of others' that cannot be taught but only exemplified (Arendt in Nixon, 2012). 'Our worst enemy is the *fear* of being creative' – choosing apathy or inertia – as 'a work of education, like a work of art, comes into being as it develops and evolves in a way that is, by definition, unforeseeable' (Dolci in Longo, 2020, p. 16).

In a 1992 project *Back to the Future*, children replicated gender and sexuality stereotypes, used gender discrimination to battle for domination

(Boys vs Girls) and, in their research 'doing', used me as evidence of the possibility of looking 'non-feminine' and being a woman with power, debating the question: *What jobs are there, where women are usually in charge?*

> Librarian, queen and princess, stripograms. (B)
> Kissograms, stripograms. If it's a man then it's got to be a woman. Unless they're gay. (B)
> When no-one else wants jobs, feminine people can get them, or gays are used. (B)
> Men think they're the breadwinners, men don't like children, women are used to them so mums do most of it, men can't stand crying children (B)
> Some mums don't trust men (G)
> You can get women football managers (G)
> A high up nurse (G)
> Not a doctor (B)
> Your mum. She wants to tidy your room. (B)
> Women wrestlers (G)
> There aren't any (B)
> You're in charge of us, so a teacher is a woman and can be in charge (G)
> So you can be feminine and the boss (G)
> NO! (B)
> You're all being sexist, they're all being sexist, Miss ... because they're saying all women are feminine and they're not- you're not, Miss, and you're in charge. (B)

There are subtle distinctions between 'listening' to children (involving them in research) and 'hearing' what they say (taking care the research benefits children in some way). Continuing to question rather than seek answers creates interspaces and acknowledges 'agential cuts' as matter and meaning operating messily together, for which we might never find definitive facts or 'truths'; a research fact of which children's playful use of irony in their drawing always teaches and reminds me. Children often interpreted who was 'the boss' at home humorously, using relative age as a mathematical marker or who bites whom (in Figure 5.12, a boy takes a stereotypically patriarchal route – Dad is boss, then himself 'because I am strong' – and tellingly ranks a Hamster higher than 'bossy Mum' or sister) or, like Ceylun in Figure 5.13, picture Mum and Dad at the top together, with consecutive cloud levels down a mountain each signed 'next', with the fish last.

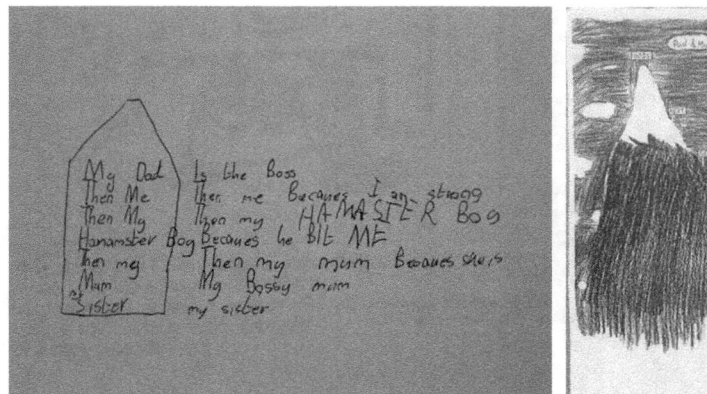 

Figure 5.12 & Figure 5.13 Children's drawings answering *Who is the boss at home?*

Relational communication is notoriously unfixed, slippery and contingent (on context, setting, language(s) visual and non-verbal cues, diverse individuals, groups and their relative roles and differences, etc.). Children are aware of and indignant about social stereotypes and injustices affecting themselves, and extending the career aspirations project into a power relations inquiry with children, we explored – through drama role-play and photographic posterworks – the nuances of relative size, gender and colour, facial expression and use of language to challenge stereotypes of control and victimization, resulting in the four posters pictured below. The two key attributes the children wanted to highlight were gender and size; both visible signs of difference, especially children's relative size being the marker for their smaller, lower, socially less significant status compared to that of 'grown-ups'. As they put it, 'we're like lower case and they're (adults) great big capital letters'.

For reasons of relationality, artworks such as these make connections across discriminatory practice (e.g. gender/size domination) but, by researching reciprocally with young children *shaping* our understandings as a continuous (unfinished) process, I have learnt that, in order not to replicate/reproduce fixed stereotypes and act as relational call for future change, the outcome must enact *playful, open questioning as art and method and research*. In this case we worked to invert the expected norms and play with assumptions or expectations, by having (for example, in poster 2: '*Are there things that men are*

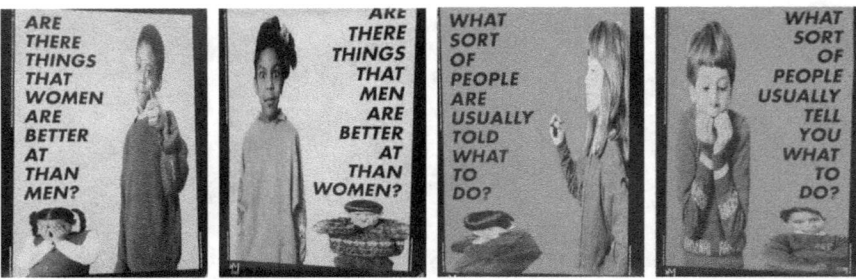

Figure 5.14 Posters created with children playfully questioning gender/power relations.

better at than women?') a Black girl dominating the frame acting assertively, with a white boy reduced in size acting meekly. In this way, the children represent their experiences as well as critique those representations; 'resisting representations', as hooks puts it in *Outlaw Culture* (2015).

The principles here are acknowledging power relations or political standpoints and being honest about 'baggage' and agendas: adult/child positionalities and those of a divided society (e.g. the recognized presence of language/identity/age/class/gender/race); thus being 'seen', and seeing research and arts education as political activism for social justice.

Academic baggage

Over the years, I have also published articles with children, first in 1995 with Ayeshea Zarcharkiw, age ten, for the journal *Children's Literature in Education*, and most recently, with Laura-Rosa Williams, age nine. The first article took the form of a conversation about Richard Hughes's novel *A High Wind in Jamaica* (1929) initially considered for children, then (possibly because of its radically modernist narrative where a female child is ultimately less moral than male adult pirates) re-marketed for adult readership (on the basis of changing cover design, blurbs and publishing strategy). Citing extracts from our discussion, I argued that Ayeshea, without what one might consider adult sexual awareness, read the significant motifs of the novel as acutely as my university students had, highly sensitive as she was to the novel's play (and inversion) of power relations. Though Ayeshea was included in forming the article's structure and content, at the time I felt that I dominated in terms of authoring the piece. Consequently, finding the right register was difficult.

The 2023 piece with Jayne Osgood and Laura-Rosa (L-R) used collaborative arts practices where the child researcher was actively agential – sometimes leading – in creating lists, object play, drawing, reading and discussing 'finding things down the back of a chair' as a research method. Whilst we were 'doing', I never doubted we were 'researching-with' a child-researcher, and our exchanges were of mutual interest and benefit. For example, L-R would often write and draw in streams-of-consciousness with admirable rapidity, encouraging the adults to be similarly present in the moment and to follow feeling, instinct and intuition. Valuing these qualities is more enjoyable and engaging – thus intrinsically motivating – for researchers of all ages, as it keeps the research thinking fresh and limits risk-adverse academic conservatism.

Object relations analysis with children avoids 'using' or working with children as (passive) *objects* of research, as we are all confronted with the complexity of ourselves as subjects playing in the world, having rights (e.g. the UN right to play – does that extend to adults?) and response-abilities, co-making meaning through our *present*, rather than *represented* participation (often a distinction for posthumanism's child). Research practices can learn from children in this respect, about the play of play and of power. In the sense that a child is no more than a description of shifting moments in time, until, as Karin Murris puts it, citing Kennedy and Kohan (2008), 'the concept "child" shifts from noun to verb', and we realize it is 'something all of us can do, to child' (Murris, 2016, p. 89).

However, once faced with 'writing up' and incorporating extracts from L-R's play, her drawings and comments into a theoretical framework that she herself would have no interest in reading or hearing about, authorship felt like an uncomfortable reminder of Haraway's 'God trick': and its seeming objectivity played out in academic articles. This stage of the research felt no longer 'with' L-R, but 'about' her; a subject to object shift. Unfortunately, this feeling is reinforced by academic review before publication often seeking hard facts (from already-established scholarly disciplines) about, for example, what kind of relationality was being described: was it perhaps an anthropological 'deep hanging out' (Geertz, 1998) or immersive observation? Or, a 'relational aesthetic intersubjective encounter' (Bourriaud, 2002)? Freire always argued that 'what should be contrasted with practice is not theory, which is inseparable from it, but *the nonsense of imitative thinking*' (Freire, 1985, p. 11; my emphasis). Somehow even having to name a relationship in already thought-out (imitative) academic terms has the effect of instrumentalizing adult/child exchanges where meaning was made collaboratively under momentarily shared conditions, and whose endpoint was unforeseeable. 'What's the relationship? It's a figment of our imaginations' is the honest answer I wished we had written.

With arts education projects, children can be included at all stages of the research, including the dissemination of whatever outcomes emerge. As Coyne and Carter point out, in this kind of participatory research, 'it does not mean the power is shared equally, but it should mean the power differential is better balanced' (2018, p. 7). I remain in doubt about children's role in academic articles, in ways that are balanced, agential or feel real to *them*.

A few things in an inconclusive conclusion (as everything is not 'in the bag')

Keeping the bag open

For Freire,

> there is no such thing as teaching without research and research without teaching. One inhabits the body of the other. As I teach, I continue to search and re-search. I teach because I search, because I question, and because I submit myself to questioning.
>
> (Freire, 2001, p. 35)

Freire had no time for a separate category of 'teacher-researchers' as, in his view, one – like the bag metaphor – contains or 'holds' the other. And for him, 'permanent openness' is the condition that makes teaching and research possible. 'Openness to approaching and being approached, to questioning and being questioned, to agreeing and disagreeing' Freire, 2001, p. 119). Seeing Le Guin's carrier-bag theory as one of revolution, Hundert (2020) points out that she refuses to allow the idea to become binary thinking, thus it stays *open*. Hundert sees the idea of continuity without resolution as one of the most important elements of the carrier bag theory:

> Conflict, competition, stress, struggle, etc., within the narrative conceived as carrier bag/belly/box/house/medicine bundle, may be seen as necessary elements of a whole which itself cannot be characterized either as conflict or as harmony, since its purpose is neither resolution nor stasis but continuing process.

As she reminds us, 'life spins out new stories every day; the structures of power can only try and fail to contain it'. The beauty of Le Guin's, Haraway's – and everyone's – bag metaphor is that it is not so much a theory, and certainly not imitative thinking, but a *storying* of our own and reciprocal practice. 'It sometimes feels', wrote Le Guin, that the old patriarchal story is 'approaching its end. Lest there be no more telling of stories at all, some of us out here … think we'd better start telling another one, which maybe people can go on with, once the old one's finished. Maybe' (Le Guin, 2019, p. 33). The old hunter-gatherer model/story is out of date, patriarchal and adult-centred. Opening up possibilities for children to tell new ones, that maybe all of us can go on with, gives us a chance. Maybe.

Lightening the bag

The writer Arundhati Roy's passionate essay exploring the brutal effects of the pandemic in India, reminds us that, while all lives are precarious, some are more precarious than others. Seeing the pandemic as a 'portal' she is aware we could go through it, 'dragging the carcasses of our prejudice and hatred, our avarice, our data banks and dead ideas, our dead rivers and smoky skies behind us'. Or, she suggests, 'we can walk through lightly, with little luggage, ready to imagine another world' (Roy in FT, 2020). Less baggage than we currently drag about in relation to writing and researching with children could similarly free us from the dead weights of academic expectation and obfuscation, or research status and competition, in pursuit of relational intelligence, shared practice and genuinely new knowledge. A lightness of being would mean tipping up the bag, emptying it out and maybe giving up on the old stories about research and childhood. Travelling light.

Posthumanist methodology invites a refocusing on the miniscule happenings within particular early childhood assemblages to provide the means of engaging in everyday happenings within early childhood that recognize young children as both agentic and relationally interdependent to the worlds in which they are located and the assemblages of which they form part (Giugni, 2012, p. 355). This aligns with feminist commitment to activate theory through embodied arts-based practices with the aim to generate knowledge differently, in order to get at ways to include children's sense of play, their voices and creative thinking, that can offer something that is theirs, to a childhood study that is all of ours.

Play/in/g/ the bag

Neither childhood nor education should ever be reduced to the discourse of academia or schooling. Pedagogical relationships exist wherever knowledge is produced, highlighting how conflicts over meaning, language, representation become symptomatic of a larger struggle over cultural authority, the role of intellectuals and artists, and the meaning of democratic public life (Giroux, 1995, p. 8). For childhood culture, play is one of those key knowledge productions.

So this would mean putting *play* in the bag as a central process of researching-with children; of acknowledging the inherent equality, diversity, openness and cheerful risk of playful methods, changing the way we write research up to exemplify those methods, and practice what we preach. Anthropology has led some key challenges, such as Atkinson's play with Congolese refugee children in Zambia, where she argued for their drawings to be considered as equivalents to academic quotes in *From Play to Knowledge* (2006). She argues that playing with children leads to 'knowledge presented in different forms – visual, embodied performative and experiential'. The challenge to all our research with children is thus how these different forms of knowledge are 'valued and translated' (Atkinson, 2006).

Thinking with le Guin's 'advice for "trying on" people and ideas in storying,' with her feminist challenge to perceiving knowledge as a gathering, not a hunting, we should give credit to the rhythms of pretend play, asking 'what if?' by gathering matter and playing around messily with spatial and symbolic relations in abstract and non-linear ways. Also – through 'as if' – we need to acknowledge that researching with children feeds all our imaginative representational abilities, curiosity, problem-solving and creative survival skills, all of which are crucial to research worth doing. 'We have known this for long enough to suggest we should have more respect for it' (de Rijke, Osgood & Williams, 2023).

Play is also an (always) unfinished process: iterative, elastic; it is 'the potentiation of adaptive variability' (Sutton-Smith, 1997, p. 231), where making *is* flexible thinking *is* change.

If we have anything in our bag at all, let it be play and change.

Figure 5.15 A page from *Supertoys: A User's Manual* offering synonyms for play; an example of a page directed at both child reader and adult/teacher user, to explore the topic across all play's dynamics.

Acknowledgements

Warm thanks to all the children, to Kahve-Society for the former arts projects and to colleagues Abele Longo and Jayne Osgood for current insights and connections.

Note

1. For Winnicott, object relations (such as toys) serve the function of mediating (as a 'transitional object') between the child and their feelings. Many children told us how, in a rage, they threw teddies down the stairs, stamped on them, damaged them, but loved them all the more (because the toys helped in surviving the feelings/rage). In Winnicottian terms, 'the subject says to the object: "I destroyed you", and the object is there to receive the communication. The subject says: "Hello object. I destroyed you. I love you. You have value for me because of your survival of my destruction of you' (D.W. Winnicott, *Playing & Reality* 1971, p. 70).

References

Atkinson, Lucy (2006). From play to knowledge: from visual to verbal? *Anthropology Matters Journal*, 8(2), 1–17.

Barad, K. (2007). *Meeting the Universe Halfway Quantum Physics and the Entanglement of Matter and Meaning*. Durham: Duke University Press.

Benton, Michael & Fox, Geoff (1985). *Teaching Literature: Nine to Fourteen*. Oxford: Oxford University Press.

Berger, John (1972). *Ways of Seeing*. London: Penguin.

Bjerke, H. (2009). 'It's the way they do it': Expressions of agency in child-adult relations at home and school. *Child Society*, 25(93), 93–103.

Bourriaud, N. (2002). *Relational Aesthetics*. Dijon: Les Presses du Réel.

Braidotti, R. (2013). Nomadic ethics. *Deleuze Studies*, 7(3), 342–59.

Brice-Heath, Shirley (2009). The deeper game: Intuition, imagination and embodiment. In M. Styles & E. Arizpe (Eds.), *Acts of Reading: Teachers, Text and Childhood*. Stoke-on-Trent: Trentham Books.

Bruner, Jerome (1960). *The Process of Education*. CA: Harvard Press.

Coyne, Imelda & Carter, Bernie (Eds.) (2018). *Bring Participatory: Researching with Children and Young People. Co-constructing Knowledge Using Creative Techniques.* Springer.

de Rijke, Victoria & Zacharkiw, Ayeshea (1995). Reinventing the child reader. *Children's Literature in Education, 26*(3), 153–71.

de Rijke, Victoria (Ed.) (1996). *Learning through Photography 5–16.* London Borough of Harrow.

de Rijke, Victoria, Osgood, Jayne, & Williams, Laura-Rosa (2023). Down the back of a chair: What can a method of scrabbling with Le Guin's Carrier Bag Theory offer conceptions of 'the child' in the Anthropocene? In *Children's Culture Studies after Childhood.* Chapter 10, pp. 154–174. London: John Benjamins Publishing.

Freire, Paolo (1985). *The Politics of Education: Culture, Power and Liberation.* New York: Bergin and Garvey Publishers.

Freire, Paolo (2001). *Pedagogy of Freedom: Ethics, Democracy and Civic Courage.* Oxford: Rowman & Littlefield.

Geertz, C. (1998). Deep hanging out. *The New York Review of Books, 45*(16), 69.

Giroux, Henry (1995). Borderline artists, cultural workers, and the crisis of democracy. In C. Becker & A. Wiens (Eds.), *The Artist in Society: Rights, Roles and Responsibilities.* Chicago: New Art Examiner.

Giugni, Miriam (2012). Becoming worldly with: An encounter with the early years learning framework. *Contemporary Issues in Early Childhood, 12*(1), 11–27.

Gomez Peña, G. (2000). *Dangerous Border Crossers.* New York: Routledge.

Hamlyn, Jessica (2017). At the intersection of education, art and activism: The case for Creative Chemistries. *Visual Inquiry: Learning & Teaching Art, 6*(2), pp. 179–189.

Haraway, D. J. (2004). *The Haraway Reader.* London: Routledge.

Haraway, D. J. (2008). *When Species Meet.* Minneapolis: University of Minnesota.

hooks, bell (2015). *Outlaw Culture.* London: Taylor & Francis.

Hughes, C. & Lury, C. (2013). Re-turning feminist methodologies: From a social to an ecological epistemology. *Gender and Education, 25*(6), 786–99.

Hundert, Anna (2020). Carrier Bag theory of revolution. Available at: https://blog.pshares.org/a-carrier-bag-theory-of-revolution/).

Jenks, C. (2005). *Childhood.* Second Edition. London: Routledge.

Kester, Grant (1999). *Dialogical Aesthetics: A Critical Framework for Littoral Art.* Available at: http://www.c-cyte.com/OccuLibrary/Texts-Online/Kester_Littoral.pdf

Klein, M. (1935). A contribution to the psychogenesis of manic-depressive states. *Int. J. Psycho-Anal., 16,* 145–74.

Lather, P. (1993). Fertile obsession: Validity after poststructuralism. *The Sociological Quarterly, 34*(4), 673–93.

Le Guin, Ursula, K. (1996). The carrier bag theory of fiction. In Dancing at the Edge of the World. New York: Labyrinth Books.

Le Guin, U. (2019). *The Carrier Bag Theory of Fiction*. London: Ignota Press.

Longo, Abele (2020). *Danilo Dolci: Environmental Education and Empowerment*. New York: Springer.

Murris, K. (2016). *The Posthuman Child Educational Transformation through Philosophy with Picturebooks*. London: Routledge.

Nixon, John (2012). *Interpretive Pedagogies for Higher Education*. London: Bloomsbury.

Osgood, Jayne, Scarlet, Red Ruby, & Giugni, Miriam (2015). Putting posthumanist theory to work to reconfigure gender in early childhood: When theory becomes method becomes art. *Global Studies of Childhood*, 5(3), 346–60.

Renold, E. & Mellor, D. (2013). Deleuze and Guattari in the nursery: Towards an ethnographic, multi-sensory mapping of gendered bodies and becomings. In R. Coleman, J. Ringrose (Eds.), *Deleuze and Research Methodologies* (pp. 23–41). Edinburgh: Edinburgh University Press.

Roy, Arundhati (2020). The pandemic is a portal. *Financial Times*. Available at: https://www.ft.com/content/10d8f5e8-74eb-11ea-95fe-fcd274e920ca.

Supertoys: A User's Manual (2008). Kahve-Society, Arnolfini and Calverts Press.

Sutton-Smith, Brian (1997). *The Ambiguity of Play*. Harvard: Harvard University Press.

Tsing, A.L. (2015). *The Mushroom at the End of the World: On the Possibility of Life in Capitalist Ruins*. New Jersey: Princeton University Press.

6

Humming a tune: Attending to 'earworms' as a more-than observational practice in fieldwork with children

Paulina Semenec
University of British Columbia

Introduction

I'm watching Owen's[1] video of himself drawing in the classroom. Because he's holding the camera in one hand, and his marker in the other, the video is mostly out of focus, moving quickly from one area on the page to his desk, the marker, and then back to his paper again (see Figure 6.1). The thing that catches my attention as I watch this video again, is his humming – it is the song he has been humming all year long. It is the song I have also found myself humming over and over again after returning home from the school.

Children often sing and hum in the classroom, yet rarely does the sonic atmosphere of the classroom become a part of fieldwork observations or get registered as 'data'. In this chapter, I attend to and take seriously a child humming/singing a popular song that dominated the classroom during my doctoral fieldwork in a grade three classroom. This song became an 'earworm,'[2] as it occupied my mind both during fieldwork, and long afterwards. The child humming in the video I describe above had a learning designation, and was often reprimanded in class for not 'paying attention', not being able to sit still, focus and so on. The sedimented discourses and knowledge(s) about 'who' this child was had been well established by the time I came into this classroom – not only by teachers and counsellors, but by the children who often went out of their way to exclude him from their play.

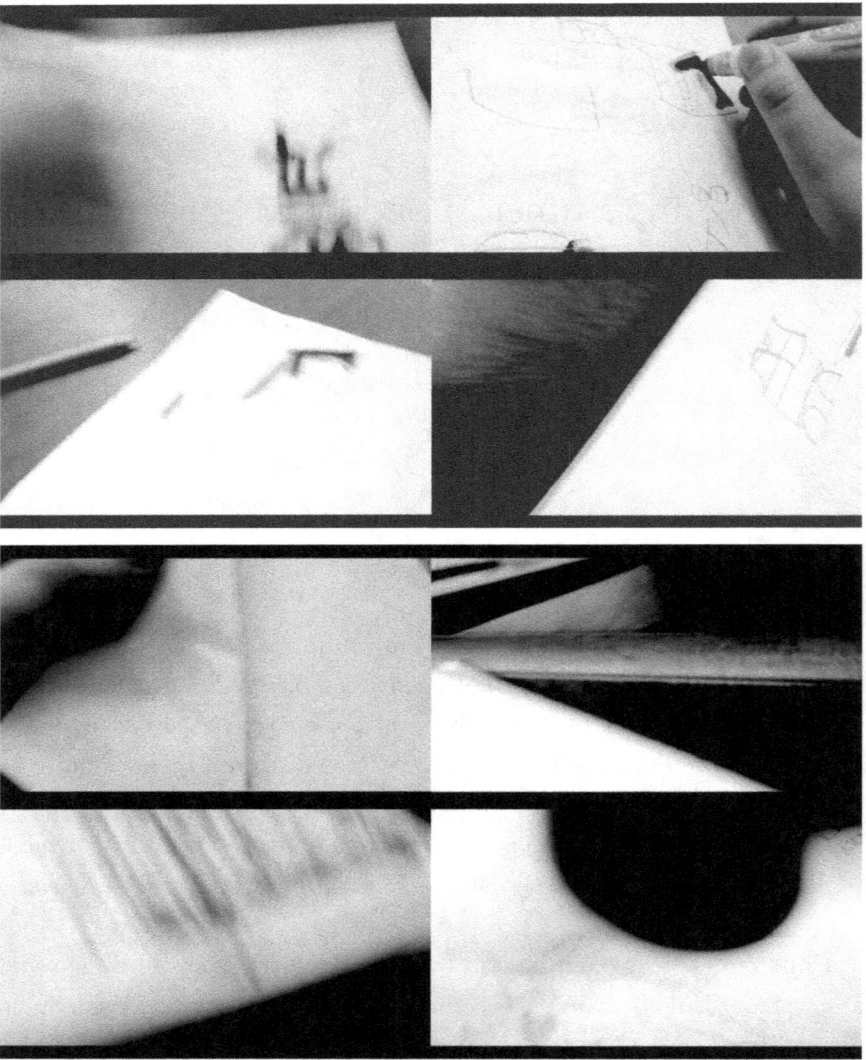

Figure 6.1 Still from Owen's video.

Informed by post-qualitative, posthuman and new materialist theories and approaches (see Diaz-Diaz & Semenec, 2020; Sakr & Osgood, 2019; Malone, Tesar & Arndt, 2020; Murris, 2016, among others), I examine how tuning in to the 'vibrational affect' (Gershon, 2013) produced by the earworm has the potential to dislodge developmentalist discourses that dominate observations in early childhood settings. In particular, I discuss how the earworm – its repetition and incoherence – offers an alternate reading of a particular child humming in a self-recorded video, one that disrupts linear narratives that claim to 'know' him. In this way, I suggest that rather than focus solely on observations of individual children's behaviours and intentions, attending to sound/earworms can make room 'for the complexities of childhood' (Blaise, 2013, p. 184) and open up more creative and equitable relations between children and researchers.

Attending to 'earworms' as (a more-than-human) observational practice

'If you're humming, you're gonna stop that now, that's very disruptive'.

As part of my doctoral research, I spent one school year in a grade 3 suburban classroom in Vancouver, British Columbia, examining children's enactments of 'mindfulness'. That is, I attended to the ways that children's attentional practices moved beyond the more conventional understandings of what it means (and looks like) to 'pay attention' as described in various textbooks and curricula (see Semenec, 2022). Like many qualitative researchers who do research in schools, I spent much of my time talking to, observing and 'hanging out' with children in the classroom, as well as in the playground, and documented many of my encounters with children through photography. Taking photographs had also quickly become something that the children in my study had become keen to do themselves, and so I had brought in an older iPhone with me to the classroom for them to use. I also noticed that some of the children had made short videos of themselves or their classmates. It was one such video – and the sound of a child humming for several minutes within it, that captured my attention, and inspires this chapter on research observation(s).

It is important to note here that I did not observe first-hand what this student (Owen) had filmed, so perhaps this is why it surprised me when I viewed it on the iPhone a few days later.[3] Owen's intense focus on his drawing coupled with his careful movements while drawing – all the while humming to himself – gave me the feeling of being 'shot in the arm' (Bennett, 2001, p. 5) – as if I was observing – and coming to know – Owen for the first time. Maggie MacLure (2016) argues that 'materialist research methodologies need to embrace the a-signifying, affective elements that are at play in becoming-child. These haunt qualitative "data" but are still often dismissed as "junk" material that distracts from truth, meaning, or authenticity' (p. 2). While Owen's humming may appear insignificant – or perhaps even disruptive, like much of children's non-verbal communication (Gallagher et al., 2017) it enchanted me, and moved me to observe the video with a renewed curiosity and openness. While not directly linked to my study, and therefore initially dismissed as insignificant 'data', I could not avoid the pull it had over me. In moving my attention to the tune Owen was humming in the video (as well as throughout the year in the classroom) rather than on Owen as an individual child, I was challenged to rethink many of the sedimented discourses that became part and parcel of how Owen came to be known by teachers (and researchers) in the school.

Taking a 'de-centered' approach to research observations with children has become the project of many scholars who think and do research with posthumanist and new materialist approaches. Such approaches (while diverse) embrace the various material-discursive entanglements that constitute children's lives including gender (Osgood, 2014; Osgood, Scarlet & Giugni, 2015; Huuki & Renold, 2016), entanglements between children and things (Allen, 2015; Myers, 2015; Pacini-Ketchabaw, Kind & Kocher, 2016), matter (Somerville & Powell, 2019), animals (Nxumalo & Pacini-Ketchabaw, 2017; Taylor & Pacini-Ketchabaw, 2017; Tammi et al., 2020; Taylor, 2020) and the spaces/places they occupy (Nxumalo, 2017; Merewether, 2019), just to name a few. Such a move towards more relational engagements has meant a break away from child-centred approaches that seek to 'know' children, such as observations and interviews. This is not to suggest that observations and interviews have no place in research with children. Rather, what many of the scholars cited above are calling for are different approaches to how we come to 'know' children – approaches that are inventive, creative, sensorial, experimental and affirmative. Of particular influence are scholars working within the umbrella of the 'reconceptualist' movement, in which a major project has been to not only critique universal and 'ideal' notions of childhood, but also to expand understandings of children and childhood in ways that move beyond discourses of development which have dominated the field of childhood studies, psychology and other social science disciplines (Burman, 2008). Within the context of education, Blaise (2013, p.184) argues that

> childhood has been rooted in developmentalism which represents childhood, teaching and learning in overly simplistic ways. Instead of making room for the complexities of childhood, developmentalism reduces these to an either/or way of thinking ... Instead of being curious about childhood and difference, developmentalism encourages teachers to determine, know and 'fix' what goes on in the classroom.

Throughout the remainder of this chapter, I experiment with short bursts of thinking/feeling/writing guided by the earworm's sonic contagion. In doing so, I wish to explore how earworms – and other sounds and noises in the classroom that may usually go unnoticed (or are silenced), can also come to matter in ways that move beyond 'data collection'. I offer three brief possibilities for earworms as a more-than-human observational practice: earworms as excess, earworms as resistance (to silence) and lastly, earworms as attachment. These three offerings are not meant to offer researchers suggestions for what to 'do' with earworm 'data'. Rather, these sections trace (in a non-linear way), the trajectory of my own thinking, being, feeling, as I surrendered to the force of the earworm, and how it altered how I came to 'know' a particular child during my research.

'Poor guy, poor guy' – earworms as excess

During the first two weeks of school, I learn that Owen has an 'R' designation which describes: 'Students requiring behaviour support or students with mental illness'. In speaking with the teacher about Owen a few months later, she tells me that he might need to go to a 'special school' next year if he doesn't improve. I note that she says 'poor guy' throughout our conversation whenever she refers to him, in an endearing kind of way. Or maybe it's pity. *Poor guy ... poor guy ...*

I am left to wonder how the refrains of teachers about children become buried inside of us, like earworms that refuse to let go – they repeat over and over, slowly and carefully reinforcing how we come to think about and 'know' particular children, and in turn, how we come to be with them through our observations and encounters. On the notion of 'excess', Willink (2010) writes that it is 'that which does not fit, does not cohere, is not logically necessary – excess baggage' (p. 207). Might the refrains of teachers also become excessive in the way they bury themselves inside us like earworms and penetrate our understandings and being with certain children?

In thinking back to my early observations of Owen, I realize that the teacher's positioning of him as a 'poor guy' informed in part, not only how I made 'sense' of his behaviour in the classroom, but also how I related to him throughout my time in the classroom. What things might we miss about children if we remain overly focused on how children are positioned by teachers and other educators in the school?

Earworms as resistance (to silence)

Children shuffle in their seats, they fidget, call out, laugh, hum and sing. In desiring stillness and quiet in the classroom, what is closed off? In the classroom, quiet is a desired state. And yet when the children were *too* quiet, it felt so unusual, that even the teacher commented on it.

In being moved by Owen's humming, I am invited to consider how this ongoing tune – this *earworm* – might open up thinking and feeling that moves us beyond the desired state of being in the classroom. In my particular research context, and perhaps like many classrooms, the desired state of being in the classroom involved quiet children who were able to regulate their emotions as well as their bodies. By demonstrating that they could sit still in their own 'personal space bubble', *some* children were awarded the teacher's praise. Others were constantly being reminded to 'sit still', 'pay attention', 'be quiet', etc. Moreover, children who experience learning or behavioural difficulties or belong to a minority group are more likely to become excluded from this desired state of being (calm, quiet, still, etc.) in the classroom.

Owen's humming – which became my personal earworm throughout the school year – subverted the desire for silence in the classroom. In particular, the earworm became a stubborn rejection of silence. Its ongoing-ness kept Owen on my mind even when I wasn't in the school, and even months (and now years later) after my research has concluded. Owen's humming overspilled the desire for silence in the classroom – his humming was a constant reminder of the ways in which we are moved towards *something* – that something catches our attention and refuses to let go. This tune became contagious, open, and porous; it affected him and me (although likely in different ways).

Earworm as attachment

The longer that Owen hums the song, the more the earworm buries itself in me. I often catch myself humming this tune – sometimes when thinking about Owen, and other times, at random moments. I don't know the lyrics to this song, but when I find out what the lyrics are, they don't seem to match Owen's humming. Was he humming his own version of this song? When I hum the tune, I don't hear my voice. I only hear Owen humming the song – frozen in time, but ongoing. Does he still hum this song too?

Jayne Osgood (this collection) posits that 'observations have capacities to re-turn us to times forgotten, transport us to other entirely unanticipated places, and to pose deeply political questions long after "data" is "collected"' p.39). It has been several years since I have seen Owen, and I no longer have connections to teachers that may know where he is today. My observation of the video where Owen is humming brings me back to a moment in time when my research was still in its early stages. I had been trained to enter a fieldwork site with a kind of 'protocol' for what and how to observe people and things, but I was unprepared for the ways that certain observations would radically shift the orientation of my research and who I was to become as a 'researcher'.

Instead of seeing Owen as unfocused, or preoccupied with something other than his school work, the earworm challenged my thinking about who Owen was (and was 'supposed to be'), and made other ways of 'knowing' him possible. Bronwyn Davies (2014) has written that 'common sense is a powerful tool that can be used to shore up the status quo, or, alternatively, it can be used to find its cracks and crevices, its potential for change' (p. 23). This video Owen made – and the humming of the song was this crack and crevice in how I came to understand Owen through the various forms of documentations and observations that followed him from a young age.

With each new line that Owen drew on the page all the while humming to himself, he was becoming something else – an attentive student focused on his art, a student able to sit still for a long time – all of the things he was deemed *not* to be able to do. Moreover, I came to view his continuous singing and apparent obliviousness to others around him not as an example of his inability to 'regulate' himself, but rather, as a kind of resistance to how he was continually being read by others. In a strange way, the repetitive nature of the earworm worked to 'speak back' against these readings – not because of the lyrics in the song, but rather, through the ways that the song always brought me back to Owen. The tenacity of Owen's voice through the earworm could not be diminished by the deficit framings of him. Moreover, in hearing his voice over and over again, I was constantly invited to re-play my own encounters with him (and observations *of* him) in the classroom, and in turn, to re-think what I thought I knew about him. In this way, I too was becoming something else. A different kind of researcher who was forced to observe differently – more carefully, slowly, mindfully.

Figure 6.2 Owen watching his video.

When the song stops playing

In thinking back to the earworm, I find it strange now that I did not consider Owen's humming important during my fieldwork. I was trained as a qualitative researcher, yet I was not sure what to 'do' with data that exceeded being 'known'. I had in some ways, disciplined myself to become an observer of things that seemed to 'matter' to the topic I was originally there to study. Perhaps over time, as so often happens whenever one spends enough time with children, one becomes moved by certain things that were once unexpected – things that may have once looked like 'nothing at all' (MacLure, 2016, p. 8). As Maggie MacLure observes: 'children and adults are caught up in events that move at different speeds and are sometimes imperceptible to one another' (*ibid*). Perhaps if such moments are to become 'perceptible', we must follow not only the material that makes it into our fieldnotes, but also that which is harder to put into words – that stuff that troubles us, moves us, affects us. This may include sounds in the classroom – humming, singing, the background/inaudible chatter of children mixed with pencils on tables, chairs moving along the floor, etc. Such sounds if given attention, may re-orient us to what else is happening, and in turn, to what *else* might come to matter to children.

In tuning in to sounds – particularly the effect/affects they produce, we can attend to not only what we observe with our eyes and ears, but also with our senses, and the affective dimensions that often come when we observe, hear, feel things that are 'imperceptible' to us. Gershon (2013) writes that '[s]ounds resonate in our bodies. They do so not only in our ears but also as something that is felt' (p. 258). Such feelings may unsettle us, as they may challenge pre-existing assumptions and practices about what and how we pay attention to children in our research. What emerges is a different picture of a 'troubled' child – one in which the child does not adhere neatly to the discourses and practices that seek to make meaning of who they 'are'. In allowing ourselves to become troubled not by our observations per se, but rather, our assumptions about what we are observing or the things we chose to intentionally leave out of our observations for the sake of producing research that matters. Ingold writes that,

> To attend to what others are doing or saying and to what is going on around and about; to follow along where others go and do their bidding; whatever this might entail and wherever it might take you … is like pushing

the boat out into an as yet unformed world – a world in which things are not ready made but always incipient, on the cusp of continual emergence. Commanded not by the given but by what is on the way to being given, one has to be prepared to wait … Indeed, waiting upon things is precisely what it means to attend to them.

(Ingold, 2014, p. 389)

While many of our research observations may be 'thoughtful' and 'principled' (Delamont, 1992), they may also be unexpected and enchanting (see Bennett, 2001) and can invite us to think and be differently with the children we research with. In letting earworms, and other sounds that may be part of the sonic atmosphere of our research setting(s), settle over time, we may become researchers who 'sing a different tune' in regards to what matters in research observations.

Notes

1 This name is a pseudonym.
2 According to Wikipedia, an earworm is: 'sometimes referred to as a brainworm, sticky music, stuck song syndrome, or, most commonly after earworms, Involuntary Musical Imagery, is a catchy and/or memorable piece of music or saying that continuously occupies a person's mind even after it is no longer being played or spoken about'.
3 Of course, there are limitations to writing about the observation of a sound/earworm. Translating any sound into text, or writing about sound in general dulls the reader's ability to become fully immersed in the experience. This chapter, however, does not seek to immerse the reader in the earworm as experienced by me, the researcher, but rather to make a claim for attending to earworms and other sounds during research observations that may make us think, be, do research in new ways.

References

Allen, L. (2015). The power of things! A 'new' ontology of sexuality at school. *Sexualities*, *18*(8), 941–58.

Bennett, J. (2001). *The Enchantment of Modern Life: Attachments, Crossings, and Ethics*. Princeton & Oxford: Princeton University Press.

Blaise, M. (2013). Activating micropolitical practices in the early years: (Re)assembling bodies and participant observations. In Coleman and Ringrose (Eds.), *Deleuze and Research Methodologies* (pp. 184–200). Edinburgh: Edinburgh University Press.

Blaise, M., Hamm, C., & Iorio, M. J. (2017). Modest witness(ing) and lively stories: Paying attention to matters of concern in early childhood. *Pedagogy, Culture & Society*, 25(1), 31–42.

Burman, E. (2008). *Developments: Child, Image, Nation*. London: Routledge.

Davies, B. (2014). *Listening to children: Being and becoming*. New York, NY: Routledge.

Diaz-Diaz, C. & Semenec, P. (2020). *Posthumanist and New Materialist Methodologies: Research after the Child*. New York: Springer Nature.

Delamont, S. (1992). *Fieldwork in Educational Settings: Methods, Pitfalls and Perspectives*. London: The Falmer Press.

Gallagher, M., Prior, J., Needham, M., & Holmes, R. (2017). Listening differently: A pedagogy for expanded listening. *British Educational Research Journal*, 43(6), 1246–65.

Gershon, W. S. (2013). Vibrational affect: Sound theory and practice in qualitative research. *Cultural Studies ↔ Critical Methodologies*, 13(4), 257–62.

Huuki, T. & Renold, E. (2016). Crush: Mapping historical, material and affective force relations in young children's hetero-sexual playground play. *Discourse: Studies in the Cultural Politics of Education*, 37(5), 754–69.

Ingold, T. (2014). That's enough about ethnography! *Hau: Journal of Ethnographic Theory*, 4(1), 383–95.

MacLure, M. (2016). The refrain of the a-grammatical child: Finding another language in/for qualitative research. *Cultural Studies ↔ Critical Methodologies*, 16(2), 173–82. https://doi.org/10.1177/1532708616639333.

MacLure, M., Jones, L., Holmes, R., & MacRae, C. (2012). Becoming a problem: Behaviour and reputation in the early years classroom. *British Educational Research Journal*, 38(3), 447–71.

Malone, K., Tesar, M., & Arndt, S. (2020). *Theorising Posthuman Childhoods*. Singapore: Springer.

Merewether, J. (2019). New materialisms and children's outdoor environments: Murmurative diffractions. *Children's Geographies*, 17(1), 105–17.

Murris, K. (2016). *The Posthuman Child: Educational Transformation through Philosophy with Picturebooks*. London: Routledge.

Myers, C. Y. (2015). *Children among Other Things: Entangled Cartographies of the More-Than-Human Kindergarten Classroom*. (Unpublished Doctoral Thesis). Ohio: Kent State University.

Nxumalo, F. (2017). Geotheorizing mountain–child relations within anthropogenic inheritances. *Children's Geographies*, 15(5), 558–69.

Nxumalo, F. & Pacini-Ketchabaw, V. (2017). 'Staying with the trouble' in child-insect-educator common worlds. *Environmental Education Research*, 23(10), 1414–26.

Osgood, J. (2014). Playing with gender: Making space for post-human childhood (s). *Early Years Foundations: Critical Issues*, 191–202.

Osgood, J., Scarlet, R. R., & Giugni, M. (2015). Putting posthumanist theory to work to reconfigure gender in early childhood: When theory becomes method becomes art. *Global Studies of Childhood*, 5(3), 346–60.

Pacini-Ketchabaw, V., Kind, S., & Kocher, L. L. (2016). *Encounters with Materials in Early Childhood Education*. New York, NY: Routledge.

Sakr, M. & Osgood, J. (2019). *Postdevelopmental Approaches to Childhood Art*. London: Bloomsbury.

Semenec, P. (2022). *'Calm's not my Style': Attending to Children's Enactments of Mindfulness in a Primary Classroom*. (Unpublished Doctoral Thesis). The University of British Columbia.

Somerville, M., & Powell, S. J. (2019). Thinking posthuman with mud: And children of the Anthropocene. *Educational Philosophy and Theory*, 51(8), 829–40.

Tammi, T., Rautio, P., Leinonen, R. M., & Hohti, R. (2020). Unearthing withling(s): Children, tweezers, and worms and the emergence of joy and suffering in a kindergarten yard. In A. Cutter-Mackenzie-Knowles, K. Malone, & E. Barrat Hacking (Eds.), *Research Handbook on Childhoodnature: Assemblages of Childhood and Nature Research* (pp. 1309–21). Switzerland: Spring Nature.

Taylor, A. (2020). Countering the conceits of the anthropos: Scaling down and researching with minor players. *Discourse: Studies in the Cultural Politics of Education*, 41(3), 340–58.

Willink, K. (2010). Excessive interviews: Listening to maternal subjectivity. *Qualitative Inquiry*, 16(3), 206–16.

7

Observing migrant children: Shifting from linguistic competence to display of agency

Federico Farini* and Angela Scollan**
University of Northampton
Middlesex University

Narratives of children's incompetence

For several decades, Childhood Studies has deconstructed mainstream narratives of childhood, particularly regarding intergenerational relationships (Qvortup, 1990; James et al., 1998; James, 2009; Oswell, 2013; Wyness, 2014; Leonard, 2016) observing that children's rights and responsibilities for constructing knowledge through interactions (defined by Heritage and Raymond (2005) as *epistemic authority*) is not promoted (Hutchby, 2007; Baraldi & Iervese, 2012), particularly in educational contexts (Scollan & Farini, 2021) because children's autonomous access to domains of knowledge (or *epistemic* status, Heritage, 2012) is downgraded by adults. As we have argued (Farini & Scollan, 2019) the epistemic status of children continues to be subordinated within adult evaluations and agendas. A narrative of children's low epistemic status and limited epistemic authority is detrimental to migrant children, particularly when difficulties in oral production are observed (Karoly & Gonzales, 2011; Harris & Kaur, 2012; Burger, 2013) and difficulties in integration are expected on the basis of cultural differences between family background and hegemonic expectations within educational settings (Farini, 2019a).

Early years education is often the first social environment where migrant children are immersed in different linguistic and cultural contexts (Pascal & Bertram, 2009; Baraldi, 2014; Scollan & Farini, 2021). Expectations of linguistic difficulties and cultural divergence may contribute to downgrading migrant children's epistemic status, favouring their inclusion as objects of adult practices, expectations, and planning (Palludan, 2007) to 'fill the gap' designed by the adult, for the child, on behalf of the child (Farini & Scollan, 2015). This promotes a discourse of 'children's needs' (Wehmeyer et al., 2017; Scollan, 2021) which is then readily translated into demands for more intensive learning, primarily second language learning, considered a precursor to active participation with teachers and peers. The investment in supporting second language acquisition can be critically approached as the consequence of the construction of migrant children as having a peculiar need for 'more education'.

Promotion of children's epistemic status

Epistemic authority is particularly limited for young children (Farini, 2019b; Murray, 2019) because of low epistemic status. Epistemic authority is further reduced for children who display difficulties in the oral production of language (Seele, 2012). When observation focuses on linguistic production, migrant children are often positioned as not-yet-competent because the focus on linguistic needs ignores children's holistic capabilities and knowledges. For migrant children who display difficulties in linguistic production, the hierarchy in epistemic status between adults and children that characterizes educational contexts (Baraldi & Corsi, 2018) and legitimizes adults' control over the trajectory and agenda of interactions (Sinclair & Coulthard, 1975; Mehan, 1979; Seedhouse, 2004; Margutti, 2006, 2010; Farini, 2011) is further reinforced. The development of specialized education for migrant children invites observation to focus on their needs rather than their interests, inviting distrust in their capabilities to actively participate in social interactions.

This troubling landscape provides a firm justification to shift the focus of research observation from linguistic competence to participation in communication. This shift describes a movement from a prescriptive model where active social participation is seen as dependent on linguistic competence, to an interest in what children *do* as they interact. Shifting the focus to social practices devotes attention to the multifaceted nature of children's participation, as celebrated in the Reggio Emilia Approach, the *Hundred Languages of Children* (Filippini & Vecchi, 1997). As a consequence, an alternative discourse of childhood that elevates children's epistemic status becomes possible (Prout, 2000; Percy-Smith, 2010; Valentine, 2011, Wyness, 2013; Baraldi et al., 2021).

Children's epistemic authority in 'Reggio Emilia Approach' (Edwards et al., 1998; Cagliari et al., 2016) positions children as active, competent and autonomous authors of knowledge (Rinaldi, 2012); observed as naturally expressive and competent agents. The Reggio Emilia Approach introduced the concept of *scuole dell'infanzia* where the ethos and methods of education are devoted to promoting children's access to the agentic status of authors of valid knowledge following a relational approach (Rinaldi, 2005; Dahlberg, 2009; Kjørholt & Qvortrup, 2012). *Scuole dell'infanzia* are underpinned by a philosophy committed to enhance all children's epistemic status and epistemic authority, as epitomized by their name: the translation of scuole *dell'infanzia* is not schools for childhood but schools *of* childhood, indicating that learning is constructed and owned by children, for children and adults. *Scuole dell'infanzia* provide an interesting site for empirical research concerned to observe the systematic elevation of children's epistemic status that promotes migrant children's active participation in social interactions even where linguistic proficiency is limited, thus offering an alternative to the discourse of children's needs and deficiencies.

Ethnomethodology and the *observations of observations*

The implications of teacher observation of/for migrant children became the subject of our research. We are interested to explore what happens when migrant children are observed as competent *communicators*, even in situations of limited linguistic proficiency. We are curious about the consequences of a shift in the focus of observation that positions migrant children as authors of valid knowledge when active participation is promoted.

Ethnomethodology allows for the observation of teachers' observations; the choice of method was underpinned by a concern to observe epistemic status and epistemic authority though an analysis of empirical sequences of actions-in-interactions. Ethnomethodology explores practical activities and practical organizational reasoning (Allen, 2017). The word 'ethnomethodology' illustrates its mission: the scientific study (-ology) of the patterned actions (-methods) of the members of a social group (ethno-) (Garfinkel, 1967). It generates detailed observations of routine, everyday affairs, the often *seen but unnoticed* social practices (Pink, 2013; Punch & Oancea, 2014) that reveal how the social order is an omnipresent feature of human life constantly reproduced through interactions (Laurier, 2009). Ethnomethodology concerns how people co-construct realities, through social interactions, based on normally unstated expectations and assumptions (Liberman, 2013). Typically, audio- or video-recordings of human activities are generated to study situated practices in close detail which are then subjected to analysis that seeks to identify particular social practices (Schatzki et al., 2001; Flick, 2015).

The choice of ethnomethodology allowed us to approach sequences of actions-in-interactions (the social practices) as empirically observable cues for the link between the positioning of migrant children vis-à-vis their epistemic status (the unstated expectations) and their access to the agentic role of authors of knowledge (the social order reproduced by interactions). It is important to clarify that observed interactions were not approached as exemplary cases of generalizable social and cultural processes. Rather, interactions were studied regarding their intrinsic properties (Creswell & Poth, 2018; Mukherji & Albon, 2018), in particular, the association between actions-in-interaction and the promotion of migrant children's epistemic authority as authors of knowledge

Over the last two decades, the traditional use of observation in education to serve the assessment of early child development against fixed learning objectives has been widely criticized (e.g. Carr, 2001; Carr & Lee, 2012; Palaiologou, 2012). This is particularly pertinent for research interested in observing how observation can promote migrant children's agency through upgrading their epistemic status and epistemic authority. The observation of observation could not be filtered by consideration of performances and levels of development (Murray & Palaiologou, 2018), for instance regarding linguistic competence. The dialogical approach to participant observation (Lawrence, 2021) was therefore chosen because it understands observation as a mutual encounter to be accomplished in and through interactions (Heath et al., 2010), and because observation is a communicative act rather than a solipsistic individual act (Markovà & Linell, 1996), where the epistemological duality 'observer and object of observation' is replaced with the acknowledgement that identities and assumptions about the world are co-constructed by continued engagement with others in an intersubjective milieu (Kabuto, 2008).

The analysis of interaction

The analysis of data produced through ethnomethodological participant dialogical observation was influenced by a conversation analytical focus on interactive achievement of meanings through sequences of actions-in-interaction. An important theoretical point for our research is that interactions can shape the context of adult-child relationships (Wingard, 2007; Gardner & Forrester, 2010), for instance contributing to the positioning of migrant children as authors of knowledge (Scollan, 2021). The analysis of data discussed in this chapter used two conversation analytical concepts: *turn-taking* and *sequence organization* (Heritage & Clayman, 2010) to investigate how the negotiation of the role of speaker (turn-taking) and the use of turn design such as questions, invitation to talk, comments, feedback on action (sequence organization) can influence migrant children's epistemic status and epistemic authority.

Although non-verbal communication may be important when children with difficulties in oral production are involved, the focus of our analysis concerns teacher's (and other children's) explicit encouragement of migrant children's authorship of knowledge, through their verbal contributions. The analytical focus on actions-in-interaction allowed the conditions that support migrant children to display their epistemic status and epistemic authority in interactions with other children and teachers to be observed, despite difficulties in speaking Italian, thus accessing the agentic status of authors of knowledge.

The research

The excerpts discussed in the following section refer to activities in *Scuola d'Infanzia* in the Province of Modena (Italy), where *programmazione* (educational planning) is influenced by the Reggio Emilia Approach. *Programmazione* underpinning the activities observed within the research was interested in promoting the *Scuola d'Infanzia* as a social space to foster the construction of children's linguistic, communicative, relational and cognitive competences in intercultural and interlinguistic contexts.

The recorded interactions involved five children of different nationalities (including Italian) across the winter term. Framed by dialogical participant observation, the research included five observations with each child. Each observation extended to a whole day of school life. Only interactions with teachers and other children were recorded, for a total running time of three hours and fifty minutes.

This chapter specifically discusses interactions recorded during observations with a four-year-old girl from Morocco (pseudonym Nadja) in the *scuola d'infanzia*. Two excerpts from transcribed interactions, involving Nadja, other children and two Italian teachers, including an *Atelierista* (the coordinator of creative workshops and art education) are presented. The excerpts analysed in the following section were selected to illustrate forms of promotion of migrant children's epistemic status and epistemic authority, connected to *the shift of observation from linguistic competence* to *participation in communication*. The English renditions of the interactions attempt to reproduce the oral production of participating children, which was conditioned by age and linguistic background.

Inspired by practices: Observing migrant children's epistemic status and epistemic authority

This section discusses three forms of interactions where migrant children's epistemic status is upgraded, and their epistemic authority is acknowledged and promoted: (1) facilitation of interactions between native and migrant children (excerpt 1); (2) negotiation of conflict between native and migrant children (excerpt 1); (3) facilitation of migrant children's epistemic status (excerpt 2).

Excerpt 1 is taken from a role-play activity where a small group of children are playing the roles of shopkeepers and customers who buy food and pay for it, inventing and negotiating prices. Two teachers (including the *atelierista*) are supervising the role-play, supporting the children in the monetary transactions and promoting their reflection on the activity.

Excerpt 1

1	Lorenzo	E il melone quello bianco, bianco
		And the melon, the white one, white
2	Nadja	Signore questo?
		Mister this?
3	Lorenzo	((moving to another stall)) Quanto quello?
		How much that one?
4	Enrico	Tre euro, mi devi dare tre euro
		Three euros, you must give me three euros
5	Lorenzo	((returns to Nadja's stall)) e il melone bianco
		And the white melon
6	Nadja	Il mellone bianco
		The white melon
7	Lorenzo	Quello
		That one
8	Nadja	Ecco
		Here it is
9	Nicola	Il melone bianco
		The white melon
10	Lorenzo	ho finito ho comprato tutto
		I'm done, I bought everything
11	Teacher	E hai pagato tutto tutto Lore? ((to other children)) dite che ha pagato tutto tutto Lore? Adesso va via ma ha pagato tutto?
		And have you paid for the whole shopping Lore) ((to other children)) you think he paid for everything everything? Now he's off but has he paid for everything?
12	Nicola	Sí
		Yes
13	Atelierista	Ma Nadja, dove sono i soldi del melone bianco?
		But Nadja, where is the white melon money?
14	Nicola	Boh
		Dunno
15	Teacher	Hai pagato la tua spesa Lore? Dico tutta?
		Have you paid for your shopping Lore? I mean all of it?
16	Atelierista	((to Nicola)) qui dal banco della frutta, dove sono i soldi di Lorenzo?
		((to Nicola)) here, at the fruit stall, where is Lorenzo's money?

17	Nadja	Dammi i soldi Lore, mi dai i soldi?
		Gimmie the money Lore, do you gimmie money?
18	Enrico	Ho scritto qui ((indicates a sheet of paper)) cosa ha comprato
		I have written here ((indicates a sheet of paper)) what he bought?
19	Lorenzo	Ho finito I soldi
		I have finished my money
20	Nadja	Sono 5 eurosoldi 5
		It's 5 euromoney 5
21	Lorenzo	Ho un grosso soldo tieni sono 5
		I have one big money, take it, it's 5
22	Nadja	Un soldo grande, ben, ciao
		A money big, goo, bye
23	Lorenzo	Avevo tanti soldi adesso non ho più
		I had lots of money now I have no more
24	Nadja	Mi ha dato i soldi!
		He has given me money!

Excerpt 1 is characterized by a conflict between Nadja and another child, Lorenzo. The conflict is provoked by the intervention of the teacher (turn 11) and the *atelierista* (turn 13) who introduce doubt that Lorenzo, who is playing the role of the customer, has not paid for his shopping in full. It is important to highlight that the Reggio Emilia Approach, as well as other pedagogical approaches, is interested in promoting children's agency, observes conflict as an opportunity to meet the other, based on the theories of conflict management that see conflict as a form of communication that can produce mutual understanding if managed dialogically (Bohm, 1996; Farini, 2014).

Excerpt 1 illustrates the idea that conflict is a form of communication rather than an obstacle against communication: the management of conflict between turn 11 and turn 24 becomes a scenario of the upgrade of Nadja's epistemic status. In the first part of the excerpt, between turns 1 and 10, Lorenzo interacts with other children, including Nadja who is playing the role of shopkeeper, as he buys some groceries. In turn 5 he asks for the *melone bianco* (white melon), which is on offer at Nadja's stall. The second part of the excerpt included the conflict, and its management led by Nadja who displays, despite a limited use of the Italian language, high epistemic status (knowledge) on the one hand, and agency with epistemic authority (expressing knowledge in the interaction) on the other hand. In turn 11, the teacher observes that Lorenzo might not have paid for all items and seems to suggest that Lorenzo did not pay for the whole shopping corroborated by the *atelierista* in turn 13. The teacher and the *atelierista* thematise the incomplete payment again in turns 15 and 16, inviting children's attention to it. Although the teacher and the *atelierista* interest in the full payment of Lorenzo's grocery shopping may appear as an adult-centred attempt to socialize children, in this excerpt it is instrumental to the promotion of children's participation, to offer an opportunity for their active participation.

In turn 17, Nadja self-selects as the next speaker, displaying agency, asking Lorenzo to pay for the *melone bianco*. Nadja's initiative is not prevented by her limited knowledge of the Italian language, and it is not made less effective, as shown by the negotiation between Nadja and Lorenzo across turns 19–24. Nadja displays high epistemic status and epistemic authority as she takes the initiative, without any external support, to initiate and lead the management of the conflict centred on payment for the *melone bianco*, until an agreement is negotiated. In excerpt 1, the intervention of the teacher and the *atelierista* creates a favourable situation for Nadja's agency. Nadja can successfully lead the management of conflict through her personal initiative, starting from the self-selection as speaker, because the adults position her as a competent participant in the interaction, acknowledging her epistemic status and epistemic authority.

Excerpt 2 illustrates an interaction that took place in the context of a small group activity.

Excerpt 2

1	Teacher	((as Nadja takes her hand and taps on her fingernails)) hai visto le mie unghie?
		Have you seen my nails?
2	Nadja	Unghi
		Nail
3	Teacher	Hai visto il colore?
		Have you seen the colour?
4	Nadja	Si blu sorella grandi
		Yes, blue sister bigga

5	Teacher	Sí?
		Yes?
6	Nadja	tanto ((pause)) tanti tela'
		Lot ((pause)) lots of tela'
7	Teacher	Oh ((to Mahmood who is standing by)) come é in Italiano? tanti
		Oh ((to Mahmood who is standing by)) how's in Italian? Lots of?
8	Aleem	tela' ((pause)) tela' azafr
		tela' ((pause)) tela' azafr
9	Nadja	tela' azfr
		tela' azfr
10	Teacher	((to Mahmood)) e come si chiama in Italiano? Cos'é?
		((to Mahmood)) and how do you say it in Italian? What is that?
11	Enrico	Cos'é?
		What is that?
12	Teacher	((to Mahmood)) hai sentito Enrico?
		Did you hear Enrico?
13	Aleem	Az a fer
		Az a fer
14	Nadja	Azfr
		Azfr
15	Teacher	Assaf?
		Assaf?
16	Aleem	Az a fer
		Az a fer
17	Teacher	Azafer
		Azafer
18	Aleem	Si ((laughs))
		Yes ((laughs))
19	Nadja	((to Mahmood, very quietly)) tel zafr
		((to Mahmood, very quietly)) tel zafr
20	Mahmood	Cosa?
		What?
21	Nadja	Tel tela' azfr
		Tel tela' azfr
22	Aleem	Cosí (imitates the gesture of varnishing fingernails))
		Like that ((imitates the gesture of varnishing fingernails))

23	Teacher	Ah, tagliaunghie
		Ah, nail clipping
24	Nadja	no taglia, é ((pause) é
		No clipping, is ((pause)) is
25	Teacher	Lima fa le unghie belle
		Nail file makes nails nice
26	Nadja	No blu fa blu
		No blue makes blue
27	Teacher	Azafer? ((to Mahmood)) ma tu sai che cosa vuole dire?
		Azafer? ((to Mahmood)) do you know what that means?
28	Mahmood	Lo so
		I know it
29	Teacher	Cosa?
		What?
30	Mahmood	Azfr é, sí, é eeee, si dice unghia s tela', si dice
		Azfr is, yeah, isssss, you say nail s tela', you say
31	Teacher	Unghie lunghe?
		Long nails?
32	Mahmood	No comeeee
		No liiiike
33	Nadja	Il colore unghi!
		The nail colours!
34	Teachers	Ecco! Il colore delle unghie, lo smalto, smalto per le unghie!
		Here it is! The nails' colour, the varnish, fingernails varnish!

The interaction is apparently initiated by Nadja. Although the theme of the interaction diverts the trajectory of the small group activity, in line with the Reggio Emilia Approach Nadja's initiative is appreciated and supported, based on the idea that children's personal initiatives are an opportunity of mutual learning, from the child, for the child, for the adults. Nadja's attention is captured by the teacher's blue nails. Rather than imposing the agenda of the activity, the teacher supports Nadja's personal initiative with a question that invites expansion (turns 1 and 3). When Nadja experiences problems in the use of the Italian language, her limited linguistic competence does not result in her marginalization and the downgrade of her epistemic status. Quite the contrary, the other participants in the interaction, the teacher and other children, take the initiative to support her, coordinated but not directed by the teacher. The agentic involvement of two Arabic-speaking children who take the initiative to support Nadja displays high epistemic status that support the access to the role of authors of knowledge who can manage the interaction autonomously.

Nadja displays agency by introducing a new, unexpected theme in the interaction through self-selection as the next speaker. The teacher supports Nadja's personal initiative with her questions that invite expansion and, even more explicitly, the teacher displays active listening and engagement with Nadja's contribution in turn 5 by interlacing a question to Nadja's previous turn 4. In turn 6, Nadia encounters a linguistic problem because she does not know the Italian word for fingernails polish (*smalto*). The first part of excerpt 2 shows that Nadja's limited knowledge of the Italian language does not prevent her agentic participation in the interaction. The second part of the excerpt, from turn 7, is characterized by the teacher's promotion of the active role of migrant children in the construction of linguistic mediation to support the ongoing interaction and narrative. In turn 6 Nadja must resort to the use of the Arabic word for fingernails polish (*tela'*, from *tela' azafer*). In turn 7, the teacher invites Mahmood who can speak Arabic to support her to understand Nadja but in turn 8 Aleem takes the initiative to self-select as next speaker, taking control of turn-taking management, which is not sanctioned by the teacher. Nadja repeats the Arabic word in turn 9, and the teacher again invites Mahmood to take the role of speaker, this time echoed by an Italian-speaking child (turn 11). Again, in turn 12 the teacher invites Mahmood to intervene. Although Mahmood is selected as the next speaker by the teacher as the recipient of the invitation, Aleem and Nadja display agency by accessing the roles of speakers, insisting on repeating *tela*, expanded in *tela' sfr (azafer)* by Nadja in turn 14. The teacher's reaction to Aleem and Nadja initiative to ignore her selection of Mahmood as next speaker is particularly interesting from an ethnomethodological perspective. The teacher's reaction to Aleem and Nadja's personal initiatives can either support their agency or impose the teacher's control over the interaction. The teacher's reaction displays, through empirically observable actions, whether Aleem and Nadja are observed as agents and whether their epistemic authority is promoted, or not. Turn 15 shows the teacher's support to Aleem and Nadja's personal initiatives: their choice to access the role of speaker is not sanctioned by the teacher. On the contrary, it is indirectly validated as the teacher tries to repeat the word *tela' sfr*. The teacher's attempt at speaking Arabic allows Aleem to claim high epistemic status as he corrects the teacher's pronunciation. In turn 17, the teacher validates Aleem's epistemic status as she accepts the correction and tries to apply it. Interestingly, Aleem's positive feedback on the teacher's response completes the three-turn sequence 'Initiation-Response-Feedback' recognized by Sinclair and Coulthard (1975), Mehan (1979), Margutti (2006, 2010), Farini (2011), Farini and Scollan (2021), among many others, as a structure of educational interaction. Nevertheless, in excerpt 2 the roles are inverted, with the child as the initiator and the evaluator of the teacher's response, making the I-R-F sequence a cue for Aleem's high epistemic status and the teacher's acknowledgement of it. In turn 19, Nadja takes another personal initiative as she selects Mahmood as the recipient of a question. However, Mahmood seems to misunderstand Nadja, triggering an extended turn in Arabic language where Nadja initiates a repair to restore mutual understanding, without much success (turn 24). In turn 26, Nadja unsuccessfully tries to explain herself in Italian. The following sequence of turns at talk is characterized by a shared commitment to restore mutual understanding, where all participants play an active role. Finally, in turn 33, Nadja finds the words to express herself in Italian, and the teacher enthusiastically displays her understanding (turn 33).

Excerpt 2 is only apparently a trivial attempt to find the Italian word for fingernails polish. If observation becomes second-order observation, focusing on teacher observations of children's position vis-à-vis their epistemic status and rights, then it is possible to appreciate that the teacher systematically promotes children's status as authors of knowledge. Throughout the interaction, the teacher validates migrant children's personal initiatives upgrading their epistemic status as 'interpreters' thus facilitating their agentic cooperation to secure mutual understanding.

Discussion and conclusion

The excerpts illustrate instances of facilitation (enhanced by teachers' initiatives), coordination (enhanced by children's initiatives) and negotiation (enhanced by both teachers and children's initiatives). Facilitation, coordination and negotiation can elevate migrant children's epistemic status, which support a higher epistemic authority as authors of knowledge; producing a change in migrant children's positioning as they access rights and responsibilities in the construction of knowledge, regardless of their linguistic competence. Such transformation is enhanced in different ways by teachers and other children. Teachers can facilitate the interaction, promoting migrant children's epistemic status and epistemic authority. Other children can actively participate in coordinated interactions and negotiations, taking initiatives that display support and appreciation.

An emphasis on improving language competence as a pre-condition for meaning participation in interaction is ancillary to dominant developmental paradigms. Such emphasis is underpinned by an approach to observation ultimately devoted to capture migrant children's needs, missing the richness of childhood experiences (Sakr & Osgood, 2019) and the knowledges that migrant children bring with them in the classroom (Baraldi, Farini & Ślusarczyk, 2022).

The excerpts show consequences of shifting observation from linguistic competences to practices of participation of communication. It challenges the link between limited linguistic competence and deficiency, inviting the promotion of children's agency through the elevation of epistemic status and epistemic authority that might promote greater inclusion. If observation focuses on children's ability to participate in interactions in unique ways (as *authentic listening*, Scollan, 2021), inclusion can be pursued as the promotion of agency thereby resisting a (re)positioning of migrant children within an ontology of troubled *childhood in deficit*.

The promotion of migrant children's agency as an upgrade of their epistemic status and epistemic authority lends itself as an alternative to scaffolding children's learning. We believe this invites reflection and further research on the impact that different approaches to observation can have on the experiences of migrant children.

References

Allen, M. (2017). Ethnomethodology. In *The Sage Encyclopaedia of Communication Research Methods*. Thousand Oaks: Sage Publications.

Baker, C. (1997) Ethnomethodological studies of talk in educational settings. In B. Davies & D. Corson (Eds.), *Oral Discourse and Education. Encyclopedia of Language and Education*. Dordrecht: Springer.

Baraldi, C. (2014). Children's participation in communication systems: A theoretical perspective to shape research. *Soul of Society: A Focus on the Leaves of Children and Youth. Sociological Studies on Children and Youth, 18*, 63–92.

Baraldi, C. & Cockburn, T. (2018). *Theorising Childhood*. London: Palgrave.

Baraldi, C. & Farini, F. (2011). Dialogic mediation in international groups of adolescents. *Language and Dialogue, 1*(2), 207–32.

Baraldi, C., Farini, F., & Joslyn, E. (Eds). (2021). *Promoting Children's Rights in European Schools. Intercultural Dialogue and Facilitative Pedagogy*. London: Bloomsbury.

Baraldi, C., Farini, F., & Ślusarczyk, M. (2022). Facilitative practices to promote migrant children's agency and hybrid integration in schools. Discussing data from Italy, Poland and England. *Language and Intercultural Communication*. DOI: 10.1080/14708477.2022.2096054.

Baraldi, C. & Iervese, V. (2012). *Participation, Facilitation, and Mediation. Children and Young People in their Social Contexts*. London/New York: Routledge.

Bohm, D. (1996). *On Dialogue*. Oxon: Routledge.

Breidenstein, G. (2008). *The Pupils' Job. An Ethnographic Approach to Schooling as Practical Accomplishment*. Paper presented on the ECER Conference 2008, Gothenburg (Paper received via author).

Buber, M. (2002). *Between Man and Man*. London: Routledge.

Burger, K. (2013). *Early Childhood Care and Education and Equality of Opportunity*. Wiesbaden: Springer.

Cagliari, P., Castegnetti, M., & Giudici, C. (2016). *Loris Malaguzzi and the Schools of Reggio Emilia: A Selection of His Writings and Speeches 1945–1993*. London: Routledge.

Carr, M. (2001). *Assessment in Early Childhood Settings: Learning Stories*. London: Paul Chapman.

Carr, M. & Lee, W. (2012). *Learning Stories: Constructing Learner Identities in Early Education*. London: Sage.

Creswell, J. & Poth, C. (2018). *Qualitative Inquiry and Research Design Choosing among Five Approaches*. Thousand Oaks: Sage.

Dahlberg, G. (2009). Policies in early childhood education and care: Potentialities for agency, play and learning. In J. Qvortrup, W.A. Corsaro & M-S. Honig (Eds.), *The Palgrave Handbook of Childhood Studies* (pp. 228–37). Basingstoke: Palgrave.

Devine, D. (2013). 'Valuing children differently? Migrant children in education. *Children and Society*, *27*, 282–94.

Doyle, W. (2006). Ecological approaches to classroom management. In W. Doyle & K. Carter (Eds.), *Handbook of Classroom Management* (pp. 97–125). London: Lawrence Erlbaum Associates.

Doyle, W. & Carter, K. (1984). Academic tasks in classrooms. *Curriculum Inquiry*, *14*(2), 129–49.

Edwards, C., Gandini, L. & Forman, G. (1998). *The Hundred Languages of Children*. Greenwich: Ablex Publishing Corporation.

Farini, F. (2011). Cultures of education in action: Research on the relationship between interaction and cultural presuppositions regarding education in an international educational setting. *Journal of Pragmatics*, *43*, 2176–86.

Farini, F. (2014). Trust building as a strategy to avoid unintended consequences of education. The case study of international summer camps designed to promote peace and intercultural dialogue among adolescents. *Journal of Peace Education*, *11*(1), 81–100.

Farini, F. (2019a). The paradox of citizenship education in Early Years (and beyond). The case of Education to Fundamental British Values. *Journal of Early Childhood Research*, *17*(4), 361–75.

Farini, F. (2019b). Inclusion through political participation, trust from shared political engagement: Children of migrants and school activism in Italy. *Journal of International Migration and Integration*, *20*(4), 1121–36.

Farini, F. & Scollan, A. (2015). *Disadvantage in the Hegemonic Discourse on Early Years Education in England. A Double-Fold Concept*. Presentation at the European Sociological Association Conference (ESA). Charles University, Prague, August 26.

Farini, F. & Scollan, A. (Eds.) (2019). *Children's Self-Determination in the Context of Early Childhood Education and Services: Discourses, Policies and Practices*. Amsterdam: Springer.

Filippini, T. & Vecchi, V. (1997). *The Hundred Languages of Children: Narratives of the Possible*. Reggio Emilia: Reggio Children.

Flick, U. (2015). Qualitative research as global endeavour. *Qualitative Inquiry*, *20*(9), 1059–63.

Gardner, H. & Forrester, M. (Eds.) (2010). *Analysing Interactions in Childhood: Insights from Conversation Analysis*. Chichester: Wiley-Blackwell.

Garfinkel, H. (1967). *Studies in Ethnomethodology*. Englewood Cliffs: Prentice-Hall.

Geier, T. & Pollmanns, M. (2016). *What Are Lessons? On the Constitution of an Educational Form*. Wiesbaden: VS-Verlag.

Glasersfeld, E. von (1987). *The Construction of Knowledge: Contributions of Conceptual Semantics*. Seaside: Intersystems Publications.

Guest, G., Namey, E., & Mitchell, M. (2013). *Collecting Qualitative Data: A Field Manual for Applied Research*. London: Sage.

Harris, F. & Kaur, B. (2012). Challenging the notions of partnership and collaboration in early childhood education: A critical perspective from a wha‾nau class in New Zealand. *Global Studies of Childhood*, 2(1), 4–12.

Heath, C., Hindmarsh, J., & Luff, P. (2010). *Video in Qualitative Research: Analysing Social Interaction in Everyday Life*. London: Sage.

Heritage, J. (2012). Epistemics in action: Action formation and territories of knowledge. *Research on Language and Social Interaction*, 45(1), 1–29.

Heritage, J. & Clayman, S. (2010). *Talk in Action. Interactions, Identities, and Institutions*. Chichester: Wiley-Blackwell.

Heritage, J. & Raymond, G. (2005). The terms of agreement: Indexing epistemic authority and subordination in talk-in-interaction. *Social Psychology Quarterly*, 68(1), 15–38.

Hutchby, I. (2007). *The Discourse of Child Counselling*. Amsterdam: John Benjamins.

James, A. (2009). Agency. In J. Qvortrup, G. Valentine, W. Corsaro, & M. S. Honig (Eds.), *The Palgrave Handbook of Childhood Studies* (pp. 34–45). Basingstoke: Palgrave.

James, A., Jenks, C., & Prout, A. (1998). *Theorizing Childhood*. Oxford: Polity Press.

Kabuto, B. (2008). Parent-research as a process of inquiry: An ethnographic perspective. *Ethnography and Education*, 3(2), 177–94.

Karoly, L. A. & Gonzales, G. C. (2011). Early care and education for children in immigrant families. *The Future of Children*, 21(1), 71–101.

Kjørholt, A. T. & Qvortrup, J. (Eds.) (2012). *The Modern Child and the Flexible Labour Market. Early Childhood Education and Care*. Basingstoke: Palgrave.

Laurier, E. (2009). Ethnomethodology/Ethnomethodological geography. In R. Kitchin & N. Thrift (Eds.), *International Encyclopaedia of Human Geography* (pp. 632–7). Oxford: Elsevier.

Lawrence, P. (2021). Dialogue Observed in Dialogue: Entering a 'Dialogical Approach to Observation' in Early Childhood. *Early Child Development and Care*, 191(2), 292–306.

Leonard, M. (2016). *The Sociology of Children, Childhood and Generation*. London: Sage.

Liberman, K. (2013). *More Studies in Ethnomethodology*. Albany: State University of New York Press.

Luhmann, N. (1995). *Social Systems*. Stanford: Stanford University Press.

Margutti, P. (2006). 'Are you human beings?' Order and knowledge construction through questioning in primary classroom interaction. *Linguistics and Education*, *17*(4), 313–46.

Margutti, P. (2010). On designedly incomplete utterances: What counts as learning for teachers and students in primary classroom interactions. *Research on Language and Social Interaction*, *43*(4), 315–45.

Marková, I. & Linell, P. (1996). Coding elementary contributions to dialogue: Individual acts versus dialogical interactions. *Journal for the Theory of Social Behaviour*, *26*(4), 353–73.

Mehan, H. (1979). *Learning Lessons*. Cambridge: Harvard University Press.

Mercer, N. & Littleton, K. (2007). *Dialogue and Development of Children's Thinking*. London/New York: Routledge.

Mukherji, P. & Albon, D. (2018). *Research Methods in Early Childhood: An Introductory Guide*. London: Sage.

Murray, J. (2019). Hearing young children's voices. *International Journal of Early Years Education*, *27*(1), 1–5.

Murray, J. (2021). Young children, rights and voice: The child's voice in research. In L. Arnott & K. Wall (Eds.), *Research through Play: Participatory Methods in Early Childhood*. London: Sage.

Murray, J. & Palaiologou, I. (2018). Young children's emotional experiences. *Early Child Development and Care*, *188*(7), 875–8.

Oswell, D. (2013). *The Agency of Children. From Family to Global Human Rights*. London: Routledge.

Palaiologou, I. (2012). *Childhood Observation for the Early Years*. Exeter: Learning Matters.

Palludan, C. (2007). Two tones: The core of inequality in kindergarten? *International Journal of Early Childhood*, *39*(1), 75–91.

Pascal, C. & Bertram, T. (2009). Listening to young citizens: The struggle to make real a participatory paradigm in research with young children. *European Early Childhood Education Research Journal*, *17*(2), 249–62.

Percy-Smith, B. (2010). Councils, consultation and community: Rethinking the spaces for children and young people's participation. *Children's Geographies*, *8*(2), 107–22.

Pink, S. (2013). *Doing Visual Ethnography*. London: Sage.

Prout, A. (2000). Children's participation: Control and self-realisation in British late modernity. *Children and Society*, *14*, 304–15.

Punch, K. F. & Oancea, A. (2014). *Introduction to Research Methods in Education*. Thousand Oaks: Sage.

Qvortrup, J. (1990). *Childhood as a Social Phenomenon an Introduction to a Series of National Reports*. Vienna: Eurosocial Report, 36/1990.

Raclaw, J. (2010). Approaches to 'Context' within conversation analysis. *Colorado Research in Linguistics, 22*. Available at: https://journals.colorado.edu/index.php/cril/article/view/295 (Last accessed: 6 January 2022).

Raymond, J. & Heritage, J. (2006). The epistemics of social relations: Owning grandchildren. *Language in Society, 35*, 677–705.

Rinaldi, C. (2005). *In Dialogue with Reggio Emilia*. London: Routledge.

Rinaldi, C. (2012). The pedagogy of listening: the listening perspective from Reggio Emilia. In C. P. Edwards, L. Gandini, & G. Forman (Eds.), *The Hundred Languages of Children: The Reggio Emilia Experience in Transformation* (pp. 233–246). Santa Barbara: Praeger.

Sakr, M. & Osgood, J. (2019). *Postdevelopmental Approaches to Childhood Art*. London: Bloomsbury.

Schatzki, T. R., Knorr-Cetina, K., & Savigny, E. v. (2001). *The Practice Turn in Contemporary Theory*. London and New York: Sage.

Scollan, A. (2021). *Facilitating children's narratives in the classroom. From self-determination to authorship of knowledge. An exploration of pedagogical innovation to promote children's agency in London primary schools*. PhD Thesis submitted to Middlesex University, 30.6.2021.

Scollan, A. & Farini, F. (2021). From enabling environments to environments that enable notes for theoretical innovation at the intersection between environment and learning. *An Leanbh Óg. The OMEP Ireland Journal of Early Childhood Studies, 14*. https://omepireland.ie/wp-content/uploads/2021/10/The-OMEP-Ireland-Journal-of-Early-Childhood-Studies.-Vol.-14-Issue-1.-2021.pdf.

Seedhouse, P. (2004). *The Interactional Architecture of the Language Classroom: A Conversation Analysis Perspective*. Oxford: Blackwell.

Seele, C. (2012). Ethnicity and early childhood. *International Journal of Early Childhood, 44*(3), 307–25.

Sinclair, J. & Coulthard, M. (1975). *Towards an Analysis of Discourse. The English used by Teachers and Pupils*. Oxford: Oxford University Press.

Tisdall, E. K. M., Davis, J. M., Hill, M., & Prout, A. (Eds.) (2006). *Children, Young People and Social Inclusion*. Bristol: Policy Press.

Valentine, K. (2011). Accounting for agency. *Children & Society, 25*, 347–58.

Wehmeyer, M. L.; Shogren, K. A., Little, T. D., & Lopex, S. J. (2017). *Development of Self-Determination through the Life-Course*. Dordrecht: Springer Nature.

Wingard, L. (2007). Constructing time and prioritizing activities in parent-child interaction. *Discourse & Society*, *18*(1), 75–91.

Wyness, M. (2013). Children's participation and intergenerational dialogue: Bringing adults back into the analysis. *Childhood*, *20*(4), 429–42.

Wyness, M. (2014). Global standards and deficit childhoods: The contested meaning of children's participation. *Children's Geographies*, *11*(3), 340–53.

8

Toddlers tinkering with toys: Following action assemblages in children's museum play

Karen Wohlwend, Yanlin Chen, and Adam Maltese
Indiana University

Introduction: children, toys and texts

We live in a media landscape populated with animated characters and narratives for young children to play. Children's media franchises carry subtle expectations for how to act as girls, boys, readers and players. For example, even a casual observer will note that children's media advertising and toy store aisles are highly gendered, filled with pink and pastel packaging to signal products for girls, metallic and neon for boys. While acknowledging that popular media is saturated with gendered, raced and classed stereotypes that are extremely problematic, an established body of literacy research shows emphatically that media depictions do not define children; instead children engage stereotypical depictions in media messages in complex ways. Despite developmental discourse that constructs children as a threatened population that is vulnerable, immature and susceptible (AAP, 2016), literacy researchers find young children are active and agentic consumers and producers of media messages (Goldstein, Buckingham & Brougère, 2005; Wohlwend, 2009; Marsh, 2014; Woods & Jeffries, 2021; Yoon, 2021).

Tinkering as child-toy-text assemblages

Postdevelopmental researchers position themselves as co-actors within a research environment, shifting from research *on* children as subjects to research *with* children. The shift here reconceptualizes a child's behaviours as *action texts* (Wohlwend, 2011), a fluid, even momentary pretence that manipulates the meanings of toys, bodies and spaces to enact pretend scenarios. Through play, children 'imagine otherwise' (Medina & Wohlwend, 2014), revising and reframing given narratives to suit their immediate purposes: altering characters, settings or storylines in order to hold a coveted toy or play a favourite character, provide a role for a friend in a play scenario and so on. The action of a child picking up and playing with a toy makes malleable its anticipated role for a certain type of player and its given actions meant to express an accompanying media narrative, in this case, a meaning inspired by Doc McStuffins toys and costumes, reassembled moment-to-moment in the intra-actions of toddlers' toy-handling and movements through space, captured on chest-mounted Go-Pro cameras.

In this chapter, very young children's action texts with toys, captured by wearable body cams, are analysed to understand how toddlers use playful tinkering with museum exhibit materials to read, enact and explore possible intra-actions and toy meanings. Tinkering is a 'maker literacy' (Scott & Wohlwend, 2017; Wohlwend, 2018) that explores the properties and possible effects of varying combinations of actions, modes and materials. The goal of tinkering is not a polished product but a testing of material's physical properties to discover their meaning potentials. The result is often a temporary combination that leaves no visible trace but reveals the play potential of materials, opens a new direction to explore or suggests a possible story action.

Consistent with posthuman approaches to early childhood learning that reject hierarchical relationships between materials and bodies, literacy researchers recognize the mutual contribution of all components in an intra-action (Kuby, Gutshall Rucker & Kirchofer, 2015; Thiel, 2015; Harwood & Collier, 2017; Daniels, 2016, 2019; Wargo, 2017, 2018; Kervin, Woods, Comber & Baroutsis, 2018). This sociomaterial perspective aligns well with postdevelopmental approaches in this volume that disrupt the discourses of childhood that privilege adults' contributions and discount children's purposes and knowledges. For example, Jackie Marsh's (2017) study of a three-year-old's play revealed that she responded to the ways media texts in the objects in her home and across multiple media platforms were interconnected through the

'Internet of Toys'. Marsh's research suggests that as young children play with popular media, they navigate a dense mix of information in assemblages where agency is shared across human actors and non-human toys.

Especially relevant to our study is Abi Hackett's (2014) mapping of two-year-olds running through a museum. Young children's pathways through museum exhibits were analysed as embodied mappable texts that revealed their understandings of materials as invitations to move as they read and responded to non-human actants such as the spatial organization of the museum or the sensory meanings of materials in the exhibit. In our study, children's movements are considered part of complex assemblages of human and non-human components that converged in playful enactments and experimentation. Playful tinkering creates assemblages of educational media content, museum designers' assumptions, and young children's desires and histories with Doc McStuffins media and familiar toys (e.g. dolls and balls), and the physical properties of materials in the museum exhibit space.

This sociomaterial analysis of toddlers' playing and tinkering with toys draws on Barad's (2003) theorization of entanglement and intra-action that is co-produced by multiple human and non-human co-actants. There is no directing agent, no pre-existing subject acting upon an object driven by a human intention and purpose. Instead, there is an unfolding action that constitutes the components, created by the contributions from all components, human and non-human.

> agency is an enactment, a matter of possibilities for reconfiguring entanglements. So agency is not about choice in any liberal humanist sense; rather, it is about the possibilities and accountability entailed in reconfiguring material-discursive apparatuses of bodily production, including the boundary articulations and exclusions that are marked by those practices.
> (Barad, Dolphjin & van der Tuin, 2012)

Characterizing actants' contributions as interactive responses rather than agency is helpful as we look for ways to be open to new configurations and possibilities that toddlers create while playing with toys and wandering through the museum. Through this lens, two things are apparent: (1)

children are actively researching their bodily actions, toys and museum space through tinkering and (2) that we as adult researchers do not observe from a distance – we participate in the intra-actions that we study as entangled components. Like the children, our observations and readings of the museum visits are constrained by and entangled with developmental discourses, design conventions and assumptions, media understanding, histories with toys and tools, embedded messages of materials and imagined possibilities.

In this chapter, we look closely at the youngest (ages one to three) children's interactions with toys in a museum exhibit space to discover:

> How do children's action texts read, enact, and reassemble the meanings of toys and materials in a museum exhibit with child-sized equipment, costumes, and toys that represent highly popular children's media?
>
> How does theorizing individual children's play interactions as assemblages reframe children's seemingly aimless actions with toys as tinkering and exploration?
>
> How do expanded research methods disrupt developmentalist constraints and deficit discourses about early childhood by entangling body cam videos, children's actions, toys and props, and media narratives in playspaces?

Unpacking components in child-toy-text assemblages

STEM media narrative: Doc McStuffins

In the United States, pre-schoolers watch animated television programmes daily, viewing programmes on public television channels as well as commercially produced programming. The youngest children make up the largest demographic of consumers of educational television. A large segment of educational programming for children focuses on teaching concepts and skills in STEM fields (i.e. science, technology, engineering and mathematics). However, televised depictions of STEM professionals have lacked diversity in gender and race. For example, scientists are stereotypically male or when female scientists are depicted, expertise is minimized (Long et al., 2010). Despite growing inclusion of more diverse characters in educational children's media, it is important to understand who leads and who follows. In this project, we sought to understand how young children at play take up active roles and practices offered in STEM media narratives.

We first wanted to identify active characters that children might know and incorporate into their play. In previous research, we looked beyond the demographics of characters to consider whether diverse characters' behaviours were actually *doing* science in STEM educational cartoons (Maltese et al., 2017). In thirty STEM-intensive episodes, we found girls were predominantly portrayed as assistants or *problem-finders* while boys were portrayed as team leaders and *problem-solvers*. Only four cartoons depicted active roles for under-represented groups in STEM fields (i.e. girls, African-Americans). Against this media landscape, an educational children's television programme that features a female lead character actually posing and solving problems seems a giant leap forward. Doc McStuffins, the main character, is a young African-American girl who turns her playhouse into a pretend clinic and plays (convincingly) a highly skilled doctor who systematically identifies, researches, diagnoses and treats the various ailments of her toy patients.

We were fortunate to find an ideal playspace for observing children freely pretending with materials in this particular media franchise: a children's museum where young children could play with toys and materials based on the media narrative in a Doc McStuffins exhibit that featured a child-sized pretend hospital and veterinary clinic. The museum's staff designed and fabricated the exhibit to appeal to an anticipated audience of families with two- to six-year-old children.

The exhibit materials were designed and built by museum staff to mimic features of a hospital and a veterinarian's clinic, with the goal of inspiring young children to engage with STEM concepts and problem-solving processes as they toured the museum with their families. We examined children's play enactments as literacy practices (e.g. pretending or tinkering), media knowledge (e.g. Doc McStuffins characters, formulaic plot elements such as each episode's check-up with a diagnosis and treatment) and STEM actions (e.g. using stethoscopes to listen, otoscopes to look) when playing with toys, props and costumes inspired by a popular media character.

Children's museum exhibit playspace and materials

The Doc McStuffins museum exhibit was composed of four familiar medical-themed rooms with child-sized plastic play equipment, predominantly in the media franchise's signature palette of pastel tones of pink, lavender and aqua:

> *Exam Room* with exam beds, outfitted with medical toys: common medical hand-held check-up instruments (e.g., stethoscope, otoscope, thermometer, inflatable blood pressure cuff). In the center is the 'Big Book of Boos-Boos', a large medical reference book that Doc consults in each episode when diagnosing and treating the toys. Children can put on a white lab coat and use the instruments to conduct check-ups on toys at each exam bed.
>
> *Operating Room* suite with four operating tables, a scrub sink, and assorted monitors. Children can press buttons to activate lights and sounds on the table and screens.
>
> *Nursery* with cribs, rocking chairs, changing tables, switched nightlights, and baby dolls. Children can dress or undress a doll, tuck it under a blanket and put it to sleep, give them a bath or feed them with a milk bottle, and turn musical nightlights on and off.
>
> *Pet Vet* clinic with grooming stations, X-ray scanner, and fish tank. Children can brush the toy animals, drop plastic balls into the tank to feed the fish, and scan the plush toy pets to diagnose and treat ailments.

Child participants

During three days at the museum exhibit, forty-four children participated in the study, ranging from toddlers to second-graders. In this chapter, we consider the data for the sixteen participants who were one-, two- or three-year-olds. Individual visits averaged about thirty minutes in length.

Children were asked a brief set of questions to identify age and gender and to see whether children had previously watched the television series and recognized the Doc McStuffins character. Parents often answered or assisted children in answering.

Go-Pro cameras

The concepts of entanglement and intra-action (Barad, 2003) enabled a more-than-human analysis of the video data to tease out tensions and resonances in the relationships among all co-actants. An implication of this theorization is that the examination of a literacy event also entangles the observer. Because our framing with a camera lens produces what we see, a chest-mounted first-person video shot by a toddler's large-motor movements untethers our perspective and opens up opportunities to see the world differently; up-close, in constant motion, with jarringly abrupt shifts in direction.

First-person video data was collected using chest-mounted Go-Pro cameras that children wore as they played with dolls, plush animals, toy medical equipment and moved from room to room in the exhibit. We collected video data with small body cameras that children wore as they visited the Doc McStuffins exhibit with their families. Chest-mounted Go-Pro cameras captured children's handling of toys during play; the first-person camera perspective also captured children's movements around the museum, pretend conversations with toys as well as talk with siblings, parents, docents and other visitors in the museum.

Nexus analysis and research team

Nexus analysis (Scollon & Scollon, 2004; Wohlwend, 2021) enabled moment-by-moment close analysis of video-recorded play intra-actions with exhibit materials. The focus on movement, gesture and actions with objects is particularly helpful for studying actions as conceptual understanding in STEM (Glauert, 2005, 2009). Of particular importance to observing early childhood activity from a postdevelopmental orientation, nexus analysis recognizes that much information is conveyed non-verbally, through coordination of human and non-human meanings, movements and materials.

To understand how toys themselves shaped children's intra-actions, exhibit photos Go-Pro videos were analysed for non-verbal messages in museum materials and exhibit space to see how they might enable or limit children's participation and their understandings of STEM concepts and media storylines in the museum space. Nexus analysis of planning sheets provided by the museum staff identified the designers' intent for the artefacts, focal artefacts and anticipated use, and discourses that justified the artefacts' presence in the exhibit. Each Go-Pro video was analysed using video analysis software (i.e. StudioCode) to identify assemblages by tracking each child's movement through the museum and instances where they paused and/or handled different materials. Beginning and endings marked an instance at a location, that is, from the time a child arrived at an exhibit station until the time they left (Figure 8.1). Toys were also tagged to mark when a child picked up and handled a particular material (Figure 8.2). Figures 8.1 and 8.2 show the video coding of a two-year-old girl's 18-minute visit, with location instances where she stopped (red cursor on the pictured scrub sink location instance) and the toys that she handled (red cursor on the plastic brush and pretend soap toys).

The video coding showed which materials attracted children, entangled them with objects and sometimes produced meaningful intra-actions. Instances with locations or toys that had extended duration or repeated returns

Figure 8.1 Tracking sequence, duration and frequency at exhibit locations.

Figure 8.2 Tracking interactions with materials (instances of hands on toys).

seemed to indicate patterns of attachment among objects, spaces and children, that is, instances when children stayed or returned repeatedly to a place or carried a favourite toy around the museum to different locations. Within these dense sites of engagement, children's actions were analysed to see how actions revealed their reading of the materials and their responding enactments. Finally, children's actual play with exhibit toys was compared to the exhibit designers' expectations for how museum visitors would use materials (often noted in exhibit planning sheets or posted in directions on the wall next to a set of materials).

Imagining otherwise through tinkering

Playing away from (adult-centric) designs

Toddlers' movements and handling of Doc McStuffins exhibit materials enacted their readings of furniture and toys as they explored what was possible in the exhibit space. Print signage, instruction sheets, directional arrows and lighting revealed designers' adult-centric focus on caregivers as readers, rather than children, revealing developmentalist assumptions that young children would need assistance to engage toys meaningfully within each station. Each station was equipped with toys matched to the expected functions within the area. For example, the nursery cribs were furnished with large baby dolls, blankets, doll clothing, toy baby bottles and small rocking chairs.

Toys and children interacted in ways consistent with designers' intentions but also in unexpected ways. Contrary to their designed purpose at a particular station, objects travelled around the exhibit as child-toy-text assemblages when children toted small portable objects like otoscopes, blood pressure measuring cuffs and scissors. These toys were carried around the exhibit, sometimes abandoned, sometimes used interchangeably as a substitute for a range of other materials (e.g. a veterinary grooming brush dropped into the Fish Tank station's ball bin instead of a ball). Children often busily and repetitively applied one object after another in multiple combinations of toys in open-ended exploration (e.g. placing an otoscope on a doll, then a thermometer, then scissors and so on). Very young children's use of toy medical equipment appeared to respond to the physical properties of the toy but sometimes to respond to caregivers' directives or enacted demonstrations, which linked back to posted signs with step-by-step directions. Rarely did we see children incorporating the mediators that designers had anticipated such as Doc McStuffins character actions, scripts or content from the programme's formulaic storylines; caregivers' readings of the exhibit's posted directions at each station; or docents' verbal explanations. Looking across museum data, it was apparent that children's lived play histories enabled immediate recognition of familiar toys such as balls or baby dolls and allowed children to easily and independently enact a toy's embedded action text. Unfamiliar toys, such as musical nightlights and other electronic devices, inspired playful tinkering and exploration rather than the expected step-by-step posted procedure that required caregiver mediation.

Most two- and three-year-olds seemed absorbed in playing with commonplace small toys (e.g. balls, dolls, baby bottles, hand-held tools) rather than simulated medical tools and furniture that involved technology-mediated equipment such as the Pet Vet X-ray scanner toy that was connected to a touchscreen. Large, moulded plastic furniture at each station enabled some movements but restricted others. Almost no toddler in the study stopped at the Pet Vet X-ray scanner or the Operating Table station. At similar stations with more complicated technology, the fixed design of large stationary equipment limited play options through sequential, didactic and close-ended procedures that prompted children to follow two- or three-step directions to produce a single outcome (e.g. a momentary light or a buzzing sound).

By contrast, popular locations like the Fish Tank or the Nursery featured many small toys such as balls with pails or baby dolls with baby bottles and blankets that could be toted away to other stations. For example, in the Fish Feeding activity at the Fish Tank station, toddlers could place plastic pails under a large spout that dispensed small plastic balls. The balls could be caught in a pail and then dumped back into the fish tank as 'fish food', over and over again. Fish Feeding was highly popular with toddlers. Dropping a ball in the fish tank produced an immediate result and allowed children to test their hypotheses to see if the results were stable or if something new would happen if materials were handled or combined differently.

However, it seemed doubtful that toddlers understood the ball filling and dropping activity as feeding fish. Across the exhibit, key explanatory elements of the design were out of eyeshot for this age group. In the Fish Feeding station, the activity that gave the ball dropping its meaning was a small photo depicting a young girl dropping a pinch of fish food into a goldfish bowl. This photo was posted about a foot or so above the hole in the tank and far above the eye level of a toddler (see Fig. 8.3). A meaningful set of relations among ball, hole in the 'fish tank', fish-feeding illustration and child were intended by designers but these were not reflected in the children's action texts.

Children's enacted readings of the 'ball' action text revealed their understandings of its physical properties as an object to drop but more often as an object to throw or roll and then chase, perhaps consistent with prior play experiences with balls. Balls were highly attractive tactilely and visually with slick surfaces and bright colours. Balls were plentiful and portable, making them easily entangled into new configurations, which could be found all over the exhibit. The 'fish food' filling station that dispensed balls kept toddlers returning, creating patterns of attachment with extended duration (e.g. a ball clutched in a hand that moved from place to place around the exhibit) and

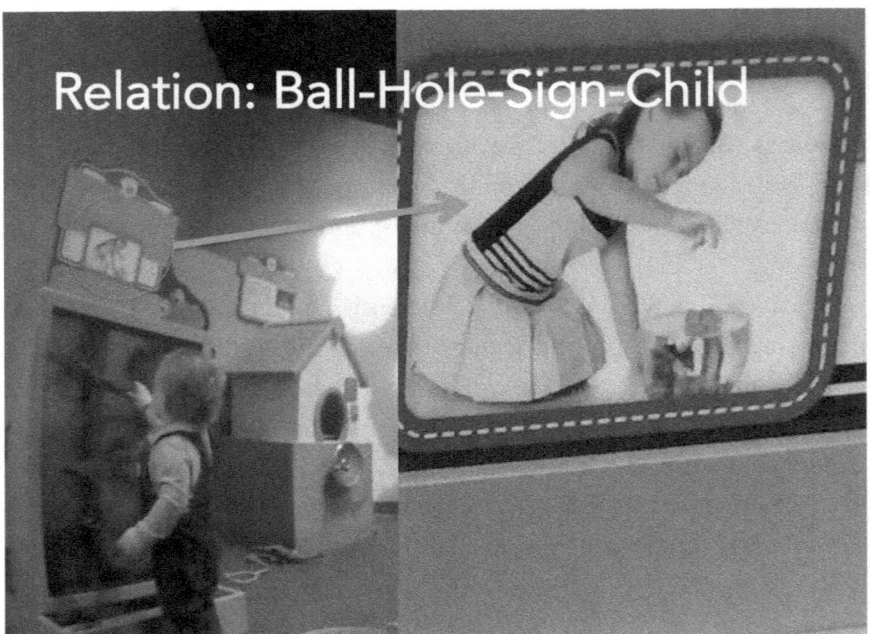

Figure 8.3 Toddler dropping a ball into the 'Fish Tank' below fish feeding image sign.

frequent repetitions and returns to ball-intensive locations (e.g. coming back again and again to the Fish Feeding station to fill a pail with balls).

Attaching to toys as co-actants

Similarly, in the nursery, baby dolls and their accessories such as bibs, blankets, milk bottles and diapers attracted and kept children engaged, toting dolls around the exhibit and returning to the Nursery location. Figure 8.4 shows the repeated loops in the trajectory of a two-year-old girl during a thirty-six-minute visit. On her first visit, after being directed by her caregivers to put the doll down and move on to another part of the exhibit, broke away from her family twice and returned in search of 'my baby' left behind in the nursery.

The relations among baby dolls, cribs, blankets and the museum space were a powerful magnet that drew children in and kept them coming back. But it also attracted accompanying adults who attached meanings to the action texts being assembled. Caregivers entered into the pretence in ways that

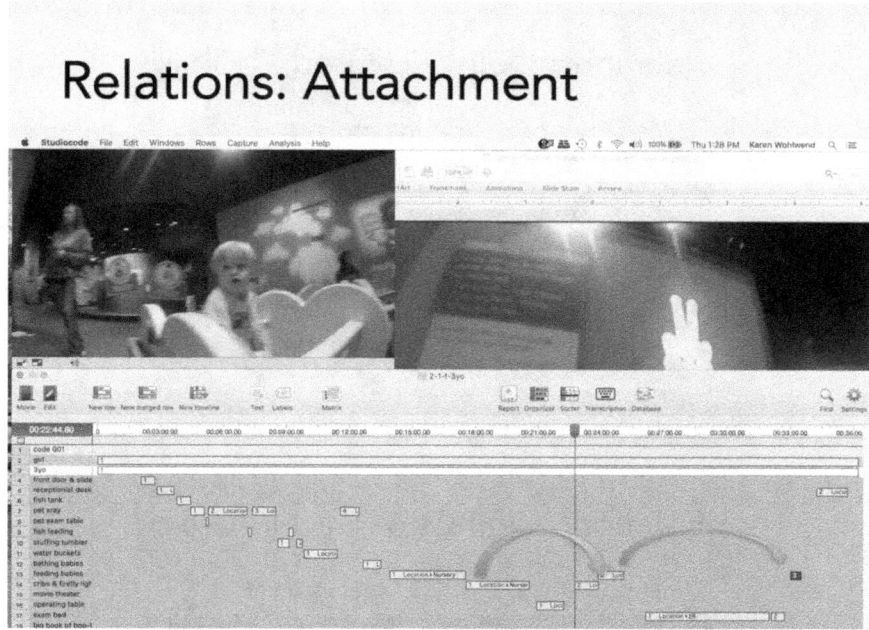

Figure 8.4 Attachment pattern: Returning to the nursery to retrieve a baby doll.

strengthened children's attachment to toys and structured relations within the child-toy-text assemblage, referring to dolls as 'your baby' or by invoking nurturing practices. When one toddler placed her doll in a crib, she first picked up a brown doll that occupied the crib and dropped it on the floor. Her mother's immediate response 'Don't put babies on the ground!' prompted the child to reconfigure the dolls-crib-child-ground relations. She immediately picked up the discarded doll, put it in a neighbouring crib, and tucked it in with a blanket before tucking in 'my baby' (Figure 8.5).

Very young children responded to materials as co-actants, talking to toys and intra-acting *with* materials as co-players rather than acting *on* objects. Caregivers often encouraged play by understanding which toys their children would prefer and directing toddlers' attention to preferred toys with a suggested action, 'Go get your baby', 'Here's a doggie' or 'Look at all the balls'. Some children quickly became attached to a toy and toted the same object from station to station until a caregiver took it away by distracting the child with alternate toy or otherwise physically separating the toy and the child. These toy attachments influenced children's movements when they sought to return

Relations: Doll-Crib-Ground-Child

- "Don't put babies on the ground"

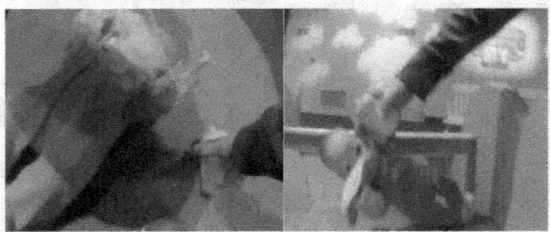

Relations: Doll-Crib-Ground-Child

- Picks up discarded doll, puts into crib

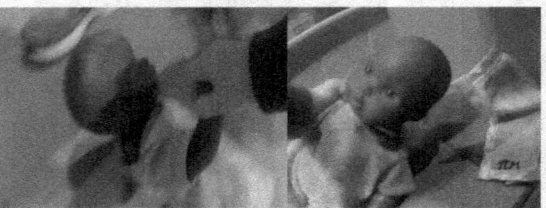

Relations: Doll-Crib-Blanket-Child

- Tucks in doll, returns to "my baby" doll

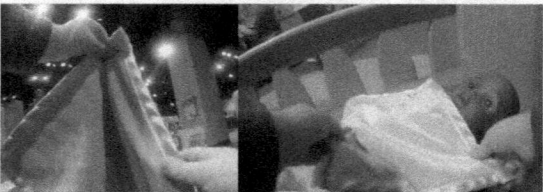

Figure 8.5 Reconfiguring doll-crib-child-ground-nurture relations.

to play with a doll in the nursery or to throw balls in the fish tank, sometimes sparking negotiations with caregivers. From an entanglement perspective, we can see that sustained attachment to a toy evidenced an emotional attraction to an object, but also a learning partnership in which a child could tinker with the play possibilities and physical properties of a toy by varying the environment to test out its meaning potential in a new setting.

Tinkering and assemblages

Sociomaterial approaches to early STEM learning such as Barad's (2003) theorization of intra-action suggest a path for rethinking early childhood concept development. In a Piagetian developmental approach to physical knowledge concept development, open-ended tinkering supports hypothesis development in young children by allowing children to test their emerging theories about physical knowledge (Kamii & DeVries, 1993). For example, after a short time, a toddler playing with a nightlight switch learns that flipping the wall switch will turn on the light and play a lullaby. Repeated experimentation will show that the child can produce the same result each time. But in Piagetian thinking, the workings of the switch are hidden and fixed, limiting the hypothesis building and learning potential.

A sociomaterial perspective on the same event reveals a two-year-old (human actant) repeatedly flicking the wall switch (non-human actant) on the Nursery nightlight. The switch is part of a larger circuit that can only be completed and activated when the switch is toggled to the on position by a human actant. The combination of human and non-human produced intra-actions that could produce two observable actions: changing the nightlight colour and simultaneously playing a melody. The co-constructed intra-action between the child actant and the switch actant created a result that creates an assemblage of child-switch-light-colour-music relations. Tinkering with toys in the museum allowed children to test their hypotheses about the material properties of the lever of the wall switch and its affordances and limits. While the underlying circuitry is black-boxed, young children could make and test hypotheses about cause-and-effect relations among fingers, switches and nightlights.

In this way, the Nursery Firefly lights offered visible and tangible intra-actions that allowed children to play with light and sound to explore the

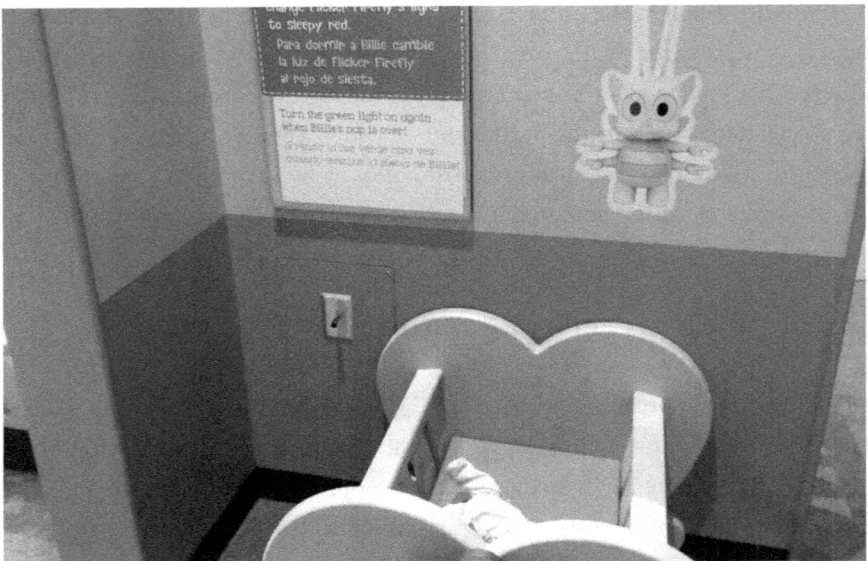

Figure 8.6 Firefly nightlight next to crib and wall switch in nursery.

properties in spontaneous experiments that were observable, replicable with reliable results and instantly responsive. Experimentation was enabled by materials that allowed children to examine the relations among components in the intra-action and to see how the configuration changed when they varied their response.

The length of time that children engaged with a toy had an impact on how much they tinkered and how robust their hypotheses or play explorations became. The key takeaway here is that the learning that comes from tinkering with toys will depend upon more than a developmental consideration of a young child's attention span or capability for reasoning. Instead, recognizing that the child is part of an entanglement opens a way to see the interdependent relationships made visible through tinkering with toys in the museum space. The toys and equipment in tinkering/play entanglement are active co-contributors in that the toy's reaction or response to the child's initiating actions produce engaging intra-actions that can support further meaning-making and hypothesizing.

How is this literacy? Elsewhere, Wohlwend (2019) has theorized tinkering as a maker literacy that reveals the meaning potential of materials and meaning variations created by physical configurations. Tinkering can reassemble components in ways that alter the material meanings of an entanglement. The intra-actions and interactions hold meaning for the child, especially when attachments to a toy and its underlying action texts are considered. Recognizing tinkering as a maker literacy enables consideration of child-made meanings that might otherwise be discounted or overlooked, meanings that are produced through and with co-actants in the brief configurations that are being made and unmade during tinkering. In early literacy research, sociomaterial research on young children's play and sense-making is expanding definitions of literacy (see for example, Thiel, 2015; Kuby & Rowsell, 2017). Additionally, the importance of children's attachment to toys in this article highlights a pressing need for more research that focuses on affect and attachment across the lifespan (Leander & Ehret, 2019).

Tinkering with developmentalist research and design

The research presented in this chapter benefited from an interdisciplinary collaboration that brought together sociomaterial perspectives on literacy research on play and science education research on materials and spaces in museums. Wohlwend's studies of play as an action-oriented literacy (Wohlwend, 2017, 2021) provided tools to read toys as texts (Wohlwend, 2009) informed by Maltese's research and development of positioning systems and methods for following embodied movement with materials and tracking relationships among spatial movement, and materials in STEM learning and experiences (e.g. Andrade, Danish & Maltese, 2017; Simpson, Anderson & Maltese, 2019). Chen's background as a student of museum administration provided a museum studies perspective on the meanings of space and materials in exhibit design. Our lenses were expanded and constrained in productive ways by our cross-disciplinary collaboration. As an interdisciplinary team, we were able to better appreciate how materials and children co-construct an action text by considering Barad's concept of intra-action as constructivist experimentation and as post-humanist entanglement.

Deveplopmentalist expectations underestimated very young children's abilities to read and respond to materials and space. Children's intentional exploration was evident in their independent navigation and novel uses of the exhibit space. Sociomaterial framing released children from the subject/agent binary to consider children as co-actants in more-than-human assemblages. Assemblages of toys, children and spaces were produced when toys attracted toddlers and toddlers responded, forming immediate attachments to toys that were tactilely or visually attractive, or that were familiar playthings or resembled beloved objects at home. Some attachments and relations that children created with the materials in the exhibit were durable and persistent, drawing children back to stations to repeat actions again and again.

Nexus analysis of Go-Pro video of children's actual engagements in the Doc McStuffins museum space located assemblages that revealed children playing beyond developmentalist assumptions in the designed environment. Evidence of developmentalist assumptions included signage that privileged verbal and pictorial explanations and procedures for exhibit stations, intended for adult guides who then would direct small children. The assumptions behind adult-centric exhibit designs underestimated very young children's abilities to read the materiality of objects and space and tinker by conducting their own explorations of the exhibit through play.

Children's attraction to and readings of materials in the museum exhibit prompted tinkering, which is conceptualized here as child-led experimentation and research that captivated toddlers but that could seem to be aimless repetition or random wandering to adults. Tinkering assemblages moved beyond the limitations and didactic directions in exhibit stations and instead featured wandering navigation and novel uses of the exhibit space. Rather than following adult-centric directions or mimicking Doc McStuffins media characters or cartoon narratives, young children played and imagined otherwise by tinkering with the physical properties of toys or replaying their prior play histories with familiar toys.

References

American Academy of Pediatrics (2016). *American Academy of Pediatrics Announces New Recommendations for Children's Media Use*. Retrieved October 21 from https://www.aap.org/en-us/about-the-aap/aap-press-room/pages/american-academy-of-pediatrics-announces-new-recommendations-for-childrens-media-use.aspx#sthash.2u6V3UQu.dpuf.

Andrade, A., Danish, J. A., & Maltese, A. V. (2017). A measurement model of gestures in an embodied learning environment: Accounting for temporal dependencies. *Journal of Learning Analytics*, 4(3), 18–46. https://doi.org/10.18608/jla.2017.43.3.

Barad, K. (2003). Posthumanist performativity: Toward an understanding of how matter comes to matter. *Signs: Journal of Women in Culture and Society*, 28(3), 801–31.

Barad, K., Dolphijn, R., & van der Tuin, I. (2012). 'Matter feels, converses, suffers, desires, yearns and remembers': Interview with Karen Barad. In R. Dolphijn (Ed.), *New Materialism: Interviews & Cartographies*. Ann Arbor: University of Michigan Press. https://quod.lib.umich.edu/o/ohp/11515701.0001.001/1:4.3/–new-materialism-interviews-cartographies?rgn=div2;view=toc.

Daniels, K. (2016). Exploring enabling literacy environments: Young children's spatial and material encounters in early years classrooms. *English in Education*, 50(1), 12–34.

Daniels, K. (2019). Movement, meaning and affect and young children's early literacy practices. *International Journal of Early Years Education*, 1–15.

Glauert, E. (2005). Making sense of science in the reception class. *International Journal of Early Years Education*, 13(3), 215–33.

Glauert, E. (2009). How young children understand electric circuits: Prediction, explanation and exploration. *International Journal of Science Education*, 31(8), 1025–47.

Goldstein, J., Buckingham, D., & Brougère, G. (2005). *Toys, Games and Media*. Mahwah, NJ: Lawrence Erlbaum.

Hackett, A. (2014). Zigging and zooming all over the place: Young children's meaning making and movement in the museum. *Journal of Early Childhood Literacy*, 14(1), 5–27. DOI:10.1177/1468798412453730.

Harwood, D. & Collier, D. R. (2017). The matter of the stick: Storying/(re) storying children's literacies in the forest. *Journal of Early Childhood Literacy*, 17(3), 336–52.

Kamii, C. & DeVries, R. (1993). *Physical Knowledge in Preschool Education: Implications of Piaget's Theory*. New York: Teachers College Press.

Kervin, L., Woods, A., Comber, B., & Baroutsis, A. (2018). Mobilising critical literacies: Text production in children's hands. *Mobile Technologies in Children's Language and Literacy: Innovative Pedagogy in Preschool and Primary Education*, 119.

Kuby C. R., Gutshall Rucker, T., & Kirchhofer, J. M. (2015). 'Go be a writer!': Intra-activity with materials, time and space in literacy learning. *Journal of Early Childhood Literacy*, 15(3), 394–419.

Kuby, C. R. & Rowsell, J. (2017). Early literacy and the posthuman: Pedagogies and methodologies. *Journal of Early Childhood Literacy, 17*(3), 285–96.

Leander, K. M. & Ehret, C. (Eds.) (2019). *Affect in Literacy Learning and Teaching: Pedagogies, Politics and Coming to Know*. London: Routledge.

Long, M., Steinke, J., Applegate, B., Knight Lapinski, M., Johnson, M. J., & Ghosh, S. (2010). Portrayals of male and female scientists in television programs popular among middle school-age children. *Science Communication, 32*(3), 356–82. https://doi.org/10.1177/1075547009357779.

Maltese, A. V., Wohlwend, K. E., Simpson, A., & McKeown, J. M. (2017, May 1). Examining Portrayals of STEM in Early Childhood Television Programming. American Educational Research Association, San Antonio, TX.

Marsh, J. (2014). Media, popular culture and play. In L. Brooker & M. Blaise (Eds.), *Sage Handbook of Play and Learning in Early Childhood* (pp. 403–14). London: Sage.

Marsh, J. (2017). The internet of toys: A posthuman and multimodal analysis of connected play. *Teachers College Record, 119*(2), 1–32.

Medina, C. L. & Wohlwend, K. E. (2014). *Literacy, Play, and Globalization: Converging Imaginaries in Children's Critical and Cultural Performances*. London: Routledge.

Scollon, R. & Scollon, S. W. (2004). *Nexus Analysis: Discourse and the Emerging Internet*. New York: Routledge.

Scott, J. A., & Wohlwend, K. E. (2017). Bringing maker literacies to early childhood education. In I. Eleá & L. Mikos (Eds.), *Young and Creative: Digital Technologies Empowering Children in Everyday Life* (pp. 209–19). Nordic Information Center for Media and Communication Research, University of Gothenburg.

Simpson, A., Anderson, A., & Maltese, A. V. (2019). Caught on camera: Youth and educators' noticing of and responding to failure within making contexts. *Journal of Science Education and Technology 28*, 480–92, https://doi.org/10.1007/s10956-019-09780-0.

Thiel, J. J. (2015). Vibrant matter: The intra-active role of objects in the construction of young children's literacies. Literacy Research: Theory, *Method, and Practice, 64*(1), 112–31.

Wargo, J. M. (2017). Rhythmic rituals and emergent listening: Intra-activity, sonic sounds and digital composing with young children. *Journal of Early Childhood Literacy, 17*(3), 392–408.

Wargo, J. M. (2018). Writing with wearables? Young children's intra-active authoring and the sounds of emplaced invention. *Journal of Literacy Research, 50*(4), 502–23.

Wohlwend, K. E. (2009). Damsels in discourse: Girls consuming and producing identity texts through Disney Princess play. *Reading Research Quarterly, 44*(1), 57–83. https://doi.org/Doi:10.1598/rrq.44.1.3.

Wohlwend, K.E. (2011). *Playing Their Way into Literacies: Reading, Writing, and Belonging in the Early Childhood Classroom*. New York: Teachers College Press.

Wohlwend, K. E. (2018, November 29). Just playing and making stuff: Children and materials as co-actants, from makerspaces to playshops. Paper presented at the annual conference of the Literacy Research Association, Indian Wells, CA.

Wohlwend, K. E. (2019, March 7). *Literacies in Motion: Reading Toys in Toddlers' Wandering and Wobbly Go-Pro Videos MakEY: Makerspaces in the Early Years*. Manchester, UK.

Wohlwend, K. E. (2021). *Literacies that Move and Matter: Nexus Analysis for Contemporary Childhoods*. London: Routledge.

Woods, A. & Jeffries, M. (2021). 'Monsters are coming!': Learning literacy and playing games. *Teachers College Record, 123*(3), online. Available at: https://www.tcrecord.org/Content.asp?ContentId=23610.

Yoon, H. S. (2018). 'The Imperial March' toward early literacy: Locating popular culture in a kindergarten classroom. *Language Arts, 95*(3), 171–81.

Yoon, H. S. (2021). Stars, rainbows, and Michael Myers: The carnivalesque intersection of play and horror in kindergarteners' (trade)marking and (copy)writing. *Teachers College Record, 123*(3), online. Available at: https://www.tcrecord.org/Content.asp?ContentId=23613.

9

'Can I draw in your sketchbook?': Collaborative observation-making with children

Hayon Park* and Jeffrey Cornwall**
George Mason University
Colorado State University

We reflect on our research through affect by exploring how it might create relations between children, materials and us, where each affect and are affected by one another, increasing our capacities to act. As we proceed with this thinking, these are the questions we consider: How might the concept of affect open up new possibilities for the ways in which observations are made with children in order to amplify the richness of childhood experiences? And, in what ways might the researcher, children and materials, like sketchbooks and pens, increase the capacities of each to observe, learn, create and research? We use a conversational format to discuss observations in early childhood research and practice as something that could be created collaboratively and emergently with children.

Traditional observation and childhood research

Often associated with empiricism, observations in research have traditionally been a dominant mode of inquiry to create valid and relevant knowledge. Empiricism is often defined by the ability to observe with the senses with much of empirical research privileging visual observation in a sense that what one has seen and felt is justified and considered reliable data. As Aune (1970) notes, empiricism is believed to require 'knowledge of matters of fact and existence to be founded on observation, memory, and inductive generalization' (p. 99). One example of the visual privilege of empiricism and observation being demonstrated in social science research is the two-way mirror where the researcher can see and observe the subjects being researched without their knowing it. The intent of the two-way mirror is to remove the gaze of the researcher, as a means to reduce variables and create a more 'objective' study. This idea of removing variables derives from the larger field of science in which research experiments are carried out in laboratories with minimal variables to create consistency in experiments. In a slightly less sterile environment, social science researchers have designed laboratories with industrial carpet, white walls, couches, books and of course, the two-way mirror. These specially designed spaces have been used to conduct research on children by codifying the observed data about children's behaviour and rendering causal relationships with their development.

Schools today often resemble a type of laboratory where children are readily accessible and can be observed by the outsider for research purposes. In her work critiquing the research methods of developmental psychology, Erica Burman (2017) notes that

> Developmental psychology was made possible by the clinic and the nursery school. Such institutions had a vital role, for they enabled the observation of numbers of children of the same age, and of children of a number of different ages, by skilled psychological experts under controlled experimental, almost laboratory conditions.
>
> (Rose, 1990, p. 142, as cited in Burman, 2017, pp. 21–2)

Ironically, the institution established for students' learning conveniently also serves the adults' desire to control and experiment on them. Though we offer approaches in our work that aim to stray away from surveillance-like observation, it is important to note that we ourselves conducted our fieldwork in such locations. We strive to be cognizant of what the institutional research setting, and traditional research methods are capable of producing. That is, regardless of the method or site, whether research becomes a disservice to children or a meaningful one is contingent on the attitude and ethical beliefs of the researcher. In other words, we believe it is not so much about the physical space or tools employed determining what observation could be, but the subtle and often unnoticed relational matters that emerge in such dynamics.

In the context of the adult researcher observing young children, it is at times assumed that the researcher's presence and the method of observing (e.g. seeing, taking field notes, engaging, etc.) rarely has an effect on how children act or behave. Burman (2017) acknowledges this myth, writing 'Observational research assumes that the act of observation does not change what it observes, a view even theoretical physics has revised, while human indeterminacy is of a different order still' (p. 171). Yet, we have come to realize that in reality this is hardly the case, if not the opposite. In our research, we noticed that children are acutely aware of our presence and performances in the classroom space and even desire to partake what the researcher intends to do. As such, we see observational research relationally, one that attends to affective matters as both the adult and child become open to the human and non-human materials.

Observation-making and childhood research

Many researchers of children use observations in their ethnographic studies (e.g. Balagopalan, 2014; Corsaro, 2003; Dyson, 2003) for its immersive, relational nature that enables one to write rich, detailed descriptions of the complex interactions between and with children. Ethnographic writing is often full of in-depth, 'thick' descriptions (Geertz, 1973) to convey the complexities and nuances of what the researcher and those they work with experience. To assist in this practice of thick description, fieldnotes are traditionally taken throughout the fieldwork to remind the ethnographer of specific events, happenings or dialogue that they experienced. While the intent is to participate in the particular culture in addition to observing, a secured time to write copious notes is often a luxury during observation. Ethnographers will occasionally step aside during or shortly after fieldwork to jot down words and ideas to remember what they are experiencing and thinking. These jotted notes assist in the thorough write ups at a later time. To write these notes, ethnographic researchers typically carry notebooks; each page usually comprises lightly coloured, horizontal lines that act as guides to keep the texts spaced out and organized.

Being artists and art educators, however, we did not carry a conventional notebook but rather a sketchbook. Unlike the notebook, a sketchbook typically contains blank pages that often weighs heavier to accommodate a variety of mediums beyond ballpoint pen and pencil. A sketchbook could not only be used for sketching, but also for painting, collage, calligraphy, mixed media and, in our case, note-taking. While it could be argued that the distinction between notebook and sketchbook is minimal, we wish to conceptualize the sketchbook as more than a book with or without lines and a methodological practice for fieldwork and fieldnotes. For instance, when children noticed our ability to draw in the sketchbook, they gradually requested more drawings from us or to draw in the sketchbooks themselves. They even aspired to use the pages in our sketchbooks as well as our pens rather than papers or pencils from the classroom. As the children participated in making marks in our sketchbooks, the notions of authorship and the purpose of sketchbook became blurred – the sketchbook offered something less determined and more fluid for both the children and us.

The appropriation of our sketchbooks from a place to write fieldnotes to a site for engaging with children's thinking, making and doing was not in fact intended. Initially, each of us attempted to adopt a traditional method of taking fieldnotes, 'accumulating written record of these observations and experiences' (Emerson, Fretz & Shaw, 1995, p. 1). As children from both classes recognized our drawing skills, what the sketchbook could do became augmented, as a site that invited children to do non-curricular activities such as drawing and experimentation with materials (e.g. the researchers' pen). Despite its seemingly ordinary matter of deviation that often occurs in school settings, we became interested in attending to the 'human matters that dominant epistemologies and interventions do not routinely conceptualize or account for' (Biehl & Locke, 2010, p. 318).

The children in the classrooms, too, seemed to recognize these as sketchbooks. By seeing that these books could be used for something more than writing, they became a prompt to also do something *more than* writing. This reminded us about how sketchbooks are considered as important provocations for children's drawing in the field of art education as

> Sketchbooks provide a bounded space for personal explorations, allowing children to pursue the themes and perfect the skills that matter most to them, to explore realities that puzzle and provoke their interest, to make

the decisions that artists make when they draw to please and inform themselves. As children formulate and follow personal projects in the pages of their sketchbooks, they learn something about themselves as artists, as individuals, and as participants in the cultures which converge and emerge in their classroom.

(Thompson, 1995, p. 7)

We wonder what this label of the sketchbook might entail for researchers and children, especially how it might lead to learning about ourselves as participants in the cultures and environment of the classroom. Moreover, in relation to research, could the sketchbook open up new possibilities for ways in which fieldwork is conducted, fieldnotes materialize and data is conceptualized?

Our experiences with the children and the sketchbooks direct us to think about childhood research differently. We consider the concept/practice of observation-making as an alternative to prescribed practices of observational research. We find Powell and Somerville's (2018) 'deep hanging out' aligning with our notions of observation-making. They describe deep hanging out as

> sitting in the sandpit and in the dirt with children, engaging with them at their level, being splashed by muddy water and being drawn into elaborate, imaginative games. It is about knowing when to be involved and when to keep your distance; when you have been included and when you have been excluded. Deep hanging out is about observing without preconceived notions of what will or should be discovered.
>
> (p. 12)

It is the unknown territory that we were eager to explore with children, even if it implied encounters of conflicts, messiness, uneasiness and other surprises. Deep hanging out resonates with Donna Haraway's (2015) curious practice in 'visiting', which 'demands the ability to find others actively interesting' on what is seemingly taken-for-granted, and 'to cultivate the wild virtue of curiosity, to retune one's ability to sense and respond' (p. 5). Haraway's elaboration of 'visiting' especially compels us as we were quite literally visitors to each classroom we observed. Through visiting, we wished to notice interesting matters about children's thinking, making and doing. As a method to attune to the complexities in the lives of children, we endeavoured to consistently activate our curiosity by visiting the classroom weekly for a prolonged period of time. It is important to note here, however, that the intention to be actively curious doesn't occur naturally nor solely by our own intentions, but with the help of children. That is, observation-making was contingent on children's acceptance of our 'visiting' our attempt to engage in a 'deep hanging out' and intimately enter their creative practices. Thanks to children's participation and invitation into their worlds, we were able to attend to observation differently, in ways that involved deliberate suspension of preconceived notions and expectations.

We also think of observation-making along with Brownyn Davies's (2014) concept of *emergent listening* where 'one must be open to being affected' (p. 20). Different from listening as usual, 'emergent listening' seeks for the 'not-yet-known' to disrupt one's judgements and prejudices, attending to 'letting go of the status quo and of the quotidian lives embedded in that status quo' (Davies, 2014, p. 28). If the conventional approach to observation aligns with listening as usual – namely, the practice of knowledge reproduction with little demands to any new thoughts to come about – observation-making attends to emergent listening, one that suspends one's ready-made knowledge and predetermined practices thus engaging in the active inquiry of new thoughts and relational matters.

Observation-making and affect

Davies's (2014) concept of emergent listening relates to Deleuze and Guattari's concept of affect, which they describe as a body's 'capacities to affect and be affected' (p. 261). Deleuze and Guattari (1987) think affect in relation to Spinoza's question 'What can a body do?' (p. 256) and discuss a body in relation to affect not only by referring to *the* body being limited to the human body, but also by including non-human bodies. Massumi (2015) specifies the relational quality of affect explaining that 'when you affect something, you are at the same time opening yourself up to being affected in turn, and in a slightly different way than you might have been the moment before' (p. 4). Thus, the capacities of a body are emergent and 'changing constantly' (Massumi, 2015, p. 4). This capacity of the body troubles the notions of a body as organism – a body as a complete whole with organs performing particular functions that determine the being of a body (see Colebrook, 2002) – and rather 'seek[s] to count its affects' (Deleuze & Guattari, 1987, p. 257). Thinking with affect makes identifying and localizing a body in one place or function difficult, as a body can have 'a thousand vicissitudes' (Deleuze & Guattari, 1987, p. 256).

Working with affect, we can think observational research and the researcher's notebook as both instruments and bodies. A notebook can be thought of as an organ of the research organism performing particular functions. In other words, a notebook is often thought of as an instrument of observational research. Through written notes, the notebook collects what is observed and creates research data. When accumulated, the contextualized data can be coded and analysed in order to find important information. In this sense, observation is something conducted onto or about the other and the relation in the observation between notebook, child and researcher resembles a unilateral form. To think of the notebook as a body that affects and is affected is to ask, 'what can a notebook do?' In our cases, thinking of the notebook affectively engaged the intense connection between the book, pen, ink, child, researcher and on and on. And because we referred to and engaged with our books as sketchbooks, it created new and different connections compared to a typical use of a notebook. Perhaps, by calling it a sketchbook, the children were more open to being affected by it as well as us. We too tried to be receptive to being affected by the children when they asked, 'Can I draw in your sketchbook?' As a result, instead of taking notes, as we had initially planned, we spent much more time drawing and making with the children. Drawing in the sketchbook produced new relations and affects with others in the classroom – both human and non-human – expanding our capacities. Deleuze (1998) writes that when bodies are open to being affected by and as well as affect the other, it increases the capacities of those bodies to act. We suggest that the curious receptiveness towards being affected by the children and materials (e.g. sketchbook, pen, etc.) increased our capacities as researchers to act and observe in the classroom.

In arguing the relational and collaborative practice of observation-making, we acknowledge that noticeable observation-making was a somewhat rare occurrence. It was often our own struggle to listen emergently and hang out deeply that created obstacles to observation-making. Though the sketchbook continued to be a material that affected many children and us, we admit that the affective relations with the sketchbook worked differently for each student.

Further, we recognize that some students chose to engage with other bodies, both human and non-human, besides the sketchbook and ourselves. Other bodies that provoked different affective relations certainly existed. Thus, it was common for us to sit aside, by ourselves and not be directly engaging with the children while they were active in schoolwork or activities. During our visits, we negotiated a back and forth between more usual practice of observation and observation-making. Through experiencing this tension, we realized that the shift to observation-making allowed us to think about what and how we are observing in the classroom and further contemplate how the altered research practice holds implications for what we can learn from/with young children.

In lieu of a traditional presentation of data, the following section presents a dialogue about how our experiences brought us together in collaborating for this chapter. It is our intent that the dialogue will allow us to speak to one another, as well as the readers, in ways that observation is imagined differently.

Stories of observation-making: A dialogue

Hayon: Jeff, remind me how our conversations about children drawing in our sketchbooks happened.

Jeff: Well, as you remember, we were sitting in that huge shopping mall connected to the convention centre in Boston, Massachusetts, USA for a national conference eating those yummy rice bowls. As we ate, you kindly asked me how my fieldwork was going. At that point I still felt quite insecure as a graduate student researcher. But since we had taken the same graduate course at Penn State about researching children a year before, I felt comfortable expressing my struggles as well as sharing some entertaining stories. I related to you my first day visiting. I brought my sketchbook to take notes in. As I sat writing and drawing, a couple students approached me to see what I was doing. I flipped through my sketchbook and soon they asked to draw inside. This request to draw in the sketchbook continued each time I visited including the insistence to use my pens. I remember how attentively you listened and then excitedly explained that your experiences were extremely similar. As we continued to give details about our work, more and more similarities emerged.

H: That's right! Those rice bowls were quite tasty. I do remember how strange and fascinating it was that our experiences were so particularly similar.

J: Remind me how it happened for you?

H: My experience was very similar. In the kindergarten classroom, my presence was inseparable from the materials that accompanied me – the spiral notebook and pen/pencil – as children were keen to notice them and the purpose of my carrying such tools. For example, in lieu of a simple 'Hi' or 'Good morning', a hurried request 'Can I draw on your sketchbook?' was by far the typical greeting I received immediately upon entering the kindergarten classroom on every visit. These materials meant for data collecting developed into an open collaborative site for drawing in which methods of ethnography leaked. In my few attempts to actually use the notebook for notetaking drew more attention and the contents were often shared. Not only the written field notes and drawings on the notebook overlapped, but also my positionality as a researcher and children's role as participants became blurred. Below are short drawing events that happened during one visit of less than two hours.

J: I'm still in disbelief that the children in both of the classrooms we visited greeted us with that same request: 'Can I draw in your sketchbook?' It makes me wonder if other researchers are having that same experience.

H: Me too. I wonder if we experienced this because our ability to draw was noticed by the children.

J: Yes, I think our rendering skills had something to do with it and even though drawing is not my forte, I still found validation when a seven-year-old looked at my drawings and asked, 'Are you an artist?' But more than our abilities to draw representationally, I wonder how our sensibilities as artists to attend and engage with the children and materials contributed to our experiences. For me, fieldwork wasn't just research. It was like a form of social art practice; the more I visited, the more I felt like a participant of the class community and less like an outside researcher.

H: I agree. How we approached observation is inseparable from our artist sensibilities.

J: How about you? Was there a particular moment when you noticed this researcher/participant binary being blurred?

H: I can recall a particular day at the preschool when I realized that my observation was no longer my own but rather something that could be shared and co-created with children. One day in February, the kindergarteners gathered around me, asking me to draw princesses of their choice. Among them, Leah asks me to draw an image of a girl she found on my iPhone, which appeared as a suggested image while browsing illustrations of Mulan on Google. I felt an instant moral panic about her choice of image because the female was not depicted in a typical princess aesthetic but rather a sexually suggestive, caricature-like illustration. The girls around us, Ayla and Sammy, even noticed that this image was different, calling it 'silly'. But when I carefully asked her why she chose the particular image, I was taken aback by her response. She simply said, 'Because it's easy to fill in'. This made me realize that the adult's aesthetic and bias about an image could be fundamentally different from what children think. Then I began asking myself: What was it about the image Leah chose that made me anxious? Who am I to discourage children from browsing, selecting and understanding images their own way? Why are adults, in general, quick to restrict children's media exposure when what they see in real life could be equally troubling? Shortly after, Austin asked me to draw Super Wings for him, which I hadn't heard of at that time. I foolishly assumed he wanted me to draw a pair of angelic wings that have superpowers embedded in it. Little did I know that Super Wings was a children's TV show about robots. It was a day that revealed my ignorance of children's culture on many levels.

J: My kids LOVE Super Wings! My son even has some action figures. It's a fun show.

H: I found this pretty interesting, so I decided to jot a note in my sketchbook. As I wrote the note, Ayla recognized Leah's name and asked, 'Where's my name?' I said, 'Right here', pointing Ayla's name from my sketchbook. She asked what I had written about Leah. I slowly read her the note. After listening carefully, Ayla asked me what the word 'image' meant. I answered that it is similar to 'a picture'. She was also curious about why I was taking notes, to which I responded, 'Because I want to keep a record of what happened and remember it'. Ayla then demands, 'You should also write about Austin'. Without hesitation, I agreed, 'Yeah, I should' and wrote Austin's name on my sketchbook page.

J: It's so interesting that Ayla directed you to write about Austin. I wonder what observations she was making about Austin to prompt her to direct you.

H: Great question. I think children are often making observations about the things around them. Children seem to be much more open to being affected and in turn to affect. Along with the children, I, too, was trying to be opened to being affected by the sketchbook, drawing practice, fieldnotes. I actually wrote about the first half of the fieldnote in much more detail in my recently published chapter without mentioning Leah's co-creation of my observation (Park, 2021), but looking back and re-reading the fieldnotes now, there are moments I wish I could have reacted or responded to differently. But the point is, observation was no longer a practice of my own but contingent on the relational matters that emerged between children and the researcher. How about you? What did observation look like for you?

J: I feel like Donna Haraway's (2015) thinking about curiosity really resonates with my experiences of observation-making in the classroom. She explains the energy needed to be open to being surprised, to the possibility that 'something *interesting* is about to happen' (p. 6, emphasis original). I tried to be excitedly interested in what might happen by (deeply) hanging out with the children. This excited interest is another way of saying that I was open to being affected by the children and materials, to listen emergently. The children too were open to being affected and in turn willing to affect the sketchbook, pens and me. Our collective openness to being affected, to listen to each other emergently, produced a practice of graphic play in the sketchbook almost every time I visited. This openness to being affected by the children and myself began spreading in the classroom beyond the sketchbook. For example, one day as the children and I were drawing in the sketchbook, I noticed Anna drawing on her hand. When she showed me her hand, clenched in a fist, she had drawn two eyes on either side of her pointer finger knuckle near the thumb. Then she drew lips to create a face. She rotated her thumb up and down so that the mouth could move and talk like a puppet. She asked if she could make a hand puppet on me. I agreed. She drew the two eyes and mouth and showed me how to move my thumb to make the hand puppet talk (Figure 9.1).

H: Haha! That's great. Did you do a puppet show?

J: Of course! The other children drawing in the sketchbook noticed what we were doing, and they drew puppets on their hands. This led to an improvised puppet show. The classroom teacher even walked by and admired our performance. Shortly after, another student noticed what

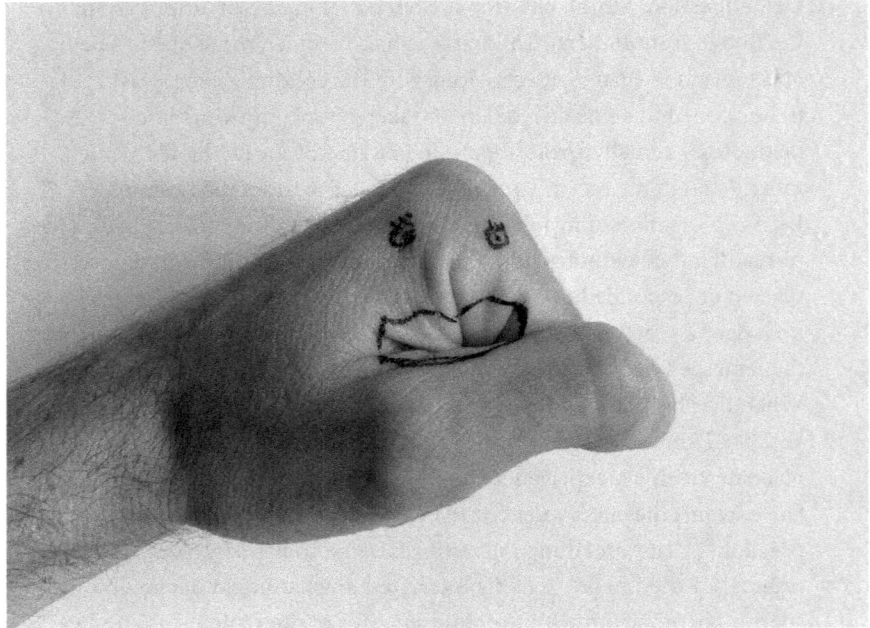

Figure 9.1 Hand puppet drawing.

we were doing and said, 'You're not supposed to draw on yourself'. As I looked at the faces of the children, they seemed to agree with her, and our performance ended. At first, our openness to being affected increased our capacities to act from graphic play in the sketchbook to puppet hand performance. But it also shows how one can be affected to decrease the capacity to act.

H: I love how the puppet show emerged. Did you often have experiences of observation-making outside of the sketchbook?

J: The request to draw in the sketchbook was fairly consistent, but as I engaged in deep hanging out and the children and I were open to being affected, we made observations together in a variety of contexts. This time during math instruction two of the children invited me to play a math card game with them. We sat on the floor, and they taught me how to play. After the first or second round, one of the children asked me to shuffle the cards. I gathered and stacked the cards, split the deck and shuffled followed by a *ripple shuffle* where the cards arch and fan back down into a single deck. The children were immediately in awe. 'Whoa! How do you do that?' I showed them again. 'Can you show us how to do that?' they implored. For the rest of the math period, we didn't play the game, but took turns shuffling cards instead. When I shuffled, I wasn't trying to distract from the math activity, but I was open for surprises, trying to attune myself to the children and materials. I am fascinated by the subjectivity of deep hanging out: What would that math instruction have looked like had I been sitting on a chair in a corner watching instead of sitting on the floor and hanging out?

H: I remember asking myself similar what-if questions too. Even though we have so many similarities in our work, I enjoy hearing about the different ways that we made observations and were affecting and being affected.

J: Your experiences are fascinating as well. I like thinking about our collaboration through affect as well. I appreciated how you were open to being affected during our conversations over rice bowls. As we talked, you listened emergently, and your openness affected me. That exchange of affect has continued throughout our work. We were making observations together as we were affecting and being affected by each other, the sketchbooks, the children, the rice bowls.

H: I agree that the exchange of affect has augmented the way I think and work with children. Now I want a rice bowl.

Reflection

Our collaboration has been surrounded by moments of affect on many levels: When we were talking over rice bowls, we were both affecting and being affected, by the meal, by each other's experience. In revisiting the conversation as a way to think, affect, be affected and to engage in practice of making-observations, we find that we were making observations together about our observational work with the children. Engaging in a dialogue, too, affected how we think about our work and opened up possibilities to present our research differently – we continued to practice emergent listening and being open to being affected and affecting during our conversations. These are a becoming that affect many parts of our lives – in and out of the classroom and in both formal and informal relations and workings.

Though ethnographic research that utilizes participant observation methods could potentiate opening up new spaces for childhood research than the disconnected two-way mirror laboratory, not all reside in affective relations. It is still subject to fall into the 'researcher knows it all' structure that limits children's voices in the research. The point being, it is not so much about the particular research method but rather the thinking and relations that the bodies actively attend to.

In this chapter, we explored how childhood observation can be something in the making, where human and non-human bodies – the children, sketchbooks, cards, digital images, etc. – are affected by each other. We consider observation differently to see how it might open up new possibilities for amplifying the mundane yet rich experiences of childhood research. In our observation making, we endeavoured to listen emergently to children and participate in the children's world. As Tim Ingold (2013) suggests, participant observation is not so much about data collection but rather an 'ontological commitment' that 'lies in the recognition that we owe our very being to the world we seek to know' (p. 5). For the researcher participating in children's world, observation is more of a committed, consistent attitude, a way of knowing from the inside and co-dependent of each other. We believe that observation-making could allow us to notice new possibilities in childhood research and offer strategies for researchers to do meaningful work. We invite you, too, to join our conversation about the continued commitment towards researching with children differently.

References

Aune, B. (1970). *Rationalism, Empiricism, and Pragmatism: An Introduction.* New York, NY: Random House.

Balagopalan, S. (2014). *Inhabiting 'Childhood': Children, Labour and Schooling in Postcolonial India.* London: Palgrave Macmillan. 237 pages. ISBN # 9780230296428

Barad, K. (2007). *Meeting the Universe Halfway: Quantum Physics and the Entanglement of Matter and Meaning.* Durham: Duke University Press.

Biehl, J. & Locke, P. (2010). Deleuze and the anthropology of becoming. *Current Anthropology, 51*(3), 317–51.

Bourriaud, N. (2002). *Relational Aesthetics.* Dijon, France: Les Presses Du Reel.

Burman, E. (2017). *Deconstructing Developmental Psychology* (3rd ed.). London: Routledge.

Colebrook, C. (2002). *Gilles Deleuze*. New York, NY: Routledge.

Corsaro, W. (2003). *We're Friends, Right?: Children's Use of Access Rituals in a Nursery School*. Washington, DC: Joseph Henry Press.

Davies, B. (2014). *Listening to Children: Being and Becoming* (1st ed.). London; New York: Routledge.

Deleuze, G. (1998). *Gilles Deleuze: Essays Critical and Clinical* (Daniel Smith and Michael Greco, Trans.). London: Verso.

Deleuze, G. & Guattari, F. (1987). *A Thousand Plateaus: Capitalism and Schizophrenia* (B. Massumi, Trans.). Minneapolis: University of Minnesota Press.

Dyson, A. H. (2003). 'Welcome to the jam': Popular culture, school literacy, and the making of childhoods. *Harvard Educational Review, 73*(3), 328–61. https://doi.org/10.17763/haer.73.3.d262234083374665.

Emerson, R. M., Fretz, R. I., & Shaw, L. L. (1995). *Writing Ethnographic Fieldnotes*. Chicago, IL: The University of Chicago Press. http://dx.doi.org/10.7208/chicago/9780226206851.001.0001.

Emerson, R. M., Fretz, R. I., & Shaw, L. L. (2011). *Writing Ethnographic Fieldnotes* (2nd ed.). Chicago, IL: University of Chicago Press.

Geertz, C. (1973). *The Interpretation of Cultures: Selected Essays*. New York: Basic Books.

Haraway, D. (2015). A curious practice. *Angelaki -Journal of the Theoretical Humanities, 20*(2), 5–14.

Ingold, T. (2013). *Making: Anthropology, Archaeology, Art and Architecture*. Routledge.

James, A., Jenks, C., & Prout, A. (1998). *Theorizing Childhood*. New York: Teachers College Press.

Massumi, B. (2015). *Politics of Affect*. Malden, MA: Polity Press.

Park, H. (2021). Queering innocence in child art: Our multiple, recurring response-abilities. In H. Park & C. M. Schulte (Eds.), *Visual Arts with Young Children: Practices, Pedagogies, and Learning* (pp. 61–72). New York: Routledge.

Powell, S. & Somerville, M. (2018). Drumming in excess and chaos: Music, literacy and sustainability in early years learning. *Journal of Early Childhood Literacy, 20*(4), 839–61.

Thompson, C. M. (1995). 'What should I draw today?' Sketchbooks in early childhood. *Art Education, 48*(5), 6–11.

Index

academic panopticon 56, 62–4, 68
accidental ethnography 42
adulthood 2
adult researcher 5, 9, 11, 13, 18, 151
affect, concept of
    body in relation to 154
    notebook/sketchbook 155
    relational quality of 154
agential questioning 83–6
Alaimo, S. 41, 44, 48, 51, 52
anthropocentric logic 26, 42, 44, 63
archive of observations 31–3
Arendt, H. 83
artists 72–3
    arts practices 76, 87
    collage/assemble 74–6
art of noticing 49
arts-based research 9, 71
arts education projects 88
Aslanian, T. K. 7, 55–68
assemblage 74–6
atmospheres 4
    and relationalities 6, 40
    and unspoken stories 27–8
attachment pattern, toys 138–41
Aune, B. 149–50
award-winning campaigns 73

Back to the Future project 83–4
baggage 86–8
    lightness of 89–90
Barad, K. 55, 57, 83, 129, 141, 143
becoming 9, 15, 29, 30, 52, 64, 76, 98, 102, 161
becoming cameras. *See* cameras observation
being there process 7, 58–9, 64. *See also* Dasein concept
being with observation 7, 14–15
borderline artists 72–3
Burman, E. 150, 151

cable-release device 74–6
cameras observation 15–16. *See also* photographic data
care, observations of 55–6, 60, 67
    photographic data and 61, 66
carrier bag theory 77, 88–9
The Carrier Bag Theory of Fiction (Le Guin) 72
Carter, B. 88
catch method 56
Chen, Y. 8, 124–44
childhood studies 1–4, 39, 45, 51, 98–9, 107
child/puddle event 28–30
    hydro-logics of water 30–1
Children's Literature in Education 86
child-toy-text assemblages 8–9, 127–44. *See also* tinkering, child-toy-text assemblages
Clark, V. 30
collage/assemble 74–6
common sense 101
community biographies 27–8
conflict, communication 114
conjoint action 83
contact zone 40
Cornwall, J. 9, 149–62
Covid-19 pandemic 29, 44–5, 50–1, 89
Coyne, I. 88
cultural worker/borderline artist educator 72–3
Cvetkovich, A. 32–3

Dasein concept 55, 56, 58–9
    and equipment 62
    nothingness and 64
Davies, B. 101, 154
deep hanging out 153–4
Deleuze, G. 64, 154, 155
de Rijke, V. 7, 71–92
developmentalism 1–2

Index

disturbances, nothingness and 60, 65
divinatory methodology 25
Doc McStuffins museum 130–2
doing nothing. *See* nothingness
doing photos observation 15. *See also* photographic data
Dreyfuss, H. 58

earworms 7–8, 95, 104 n.2
    as attachment 101–2
    data collection 99
    as excess 99–100
    as observational practice 97–9
    as resistance (to silence) 100–1
    vibrational affect 96
educational technology 8
Ehn, B. 66
emergent listening 154
empiricism 149–50
empowerment 83
emptiness. *See* nothingness
entanglement
    and intra-action 129, 133
    toys and equipment 142–3
    visual methodologies with children 17–18, 49, 98
epistemic status/authority of migrant children 108–9, 112–20
equipment
    and doing nothing 60–1
    human relationship with 55–9
    'withdrawn-ness' of 59–60
ethnomethodology/ethnographic studies 109–11, 151

Farini, F. 8, 107–20
Fawcett Society Award Winner 73
feminist new materialism 40–2, 48
Firefly nightlight 141–2
Foucault, M.
    instrument of thought 67–8
    panopticon 62–3
Freire, P. 73, 83, 88–9
futurity, questioning children 76

gender discrimination 83–6
gender-free toy design 73, 82
Gershon, W. S. 103
Giroux, H. 72–3

Giugni, M. 71
Glissant, E. 25
Go-Pro cameras 133
    Nexus analysis of 133–4
Guattari, F. 64, 154

Hackett, A. 6, 23–35, 129
Haraway, D. J. 42, 48–9, 57–8, 87, 153
Heidegger, M. 55
    Dasein concept 55, 56, 58–9, 62, 64
    on human relationship with equipment 55–9
    'withdrawn-ness' of equipment 59–60
A High Wind in Jamaica (Hughes) 86
humans and equipment 55–9. *See also* Dasein concept
humming/singing of children 95, 97–8, 100–2
Hundert, A. 88–9
Hundred Languages of Children 108–9

I/eye of childhood observation 4
image-data 12, 18. *See also* photographic data; visual data generation
    humanist hauntology of 17–19
Ingold, T. 103–4
Internet of Toys 129
Involuntary Musical Imagery 104 n.2

Jones, L. 28

The Kindergarten Book (Meyer) 16
Klein, M. 78
knowledge productions 90

Lather, P. 12
Le Guin, U. K. 72, 80, 82
    Carrier Bag Theory of Fiction 7, 72, 88–9
Let Toys Be Toys campaigns 73
lightness of baggage 89–90
linguistic competence 8, 107–9, 112, 117–18, 120
listening/hearing to children 84
Löfgren, O. 66

MacLure, M. 23–35, 98, 103
MacRae, C. 6, 23

Malabou, C. 56, 57
male gaze in photography 74
Maltese, A. 8, 124–44
Manning, E. 52
Marsh, J. 128–9
Massumi, B. 154
material memoir 6–9, 41
    Covid-19 pandemic 44–5, 51
    of feminist researcher 42–5
    Mulberry Bush nursery, picturebook 43–4
    mutated modest witnesses 51
    personal history, narratives of 40–1
    researcherly self 50
    routine and everyday happenings 48–50
    transcorporeality of 41, 52
Mazzei, L. 19
media 127
    STEM media 130–1
methodological instrumentality 11
methodological tools
    catch method 56
    plastic reading method 57
    recycling research 56–8
migrant children 107
    as competent communicators 109
    epistemic status/authority 108–9, 112–19
    linguistic and cultural contexts 107–8
    non-verbal communication 111
    recorded interactions 112
    sequence organization 111
mind's-eye images 30–1, 33–4
more-than-human worlds research 64, 67, 68
    attending to earworms 97–102
multi-sensory observations 4
Murris, Karin 87
museum 132
    and children's learning/engagement 26–7, 32
    Doc McStuffins 130–1
    playspace and materials 132
music-making services 45
mutated modest witness 42, 49, 50
Myers, C. 5, 11–19
    The Kindergarten Book 16

Neimanis, A. 30, 31
Nexus analysis 133–5
Noble, K. 27
non-verbal communication 111
Nordstrom, S. N. 64, 65
nothingness 55, 64–7
    equipment failure and 60–1
    photographic data and 66
Nursery Firefly lights 141–2
nursery observations 42–5

object relations theory 78–81, 92 n.1
    analysis with children 87
observation-making 9
    and affect 154–6
    and childhood research 151–4
    stories of 156–61
observations of children 1, 39–40
    being with 7, 14–15
    in Dasein 59 (*see also* Dasein concept)
    de-centered approach 98
    doing photos 15
    empiricism and 149–50
    I/eye of 4
    with ironstone 26–8
    on linguistic competence 108–9, 112, 117–18, 120
    multi-sensory 4
    nothingness 55, 60–1, 64–7
    at the nurseries 42–5
    as queer archive 31–3
    sense of the child 6
observing-then-reading 6, 23–5, 34
    archive of observations 31–3
    child/puddle event 28–30, 34
    community biographies 27–8
    idea of opacity 25
    museum and children's learning 26–7
opacity 25
Osgood, J. 6–7, 39–52, 87, 101
Outlaw Culture (hooks) 86

Pacini-Ketchabaw, V. 30
Park, H. 9, 149–62
partial perspectives 42

participant observer 14
Penfield, C. 64
personal expressions 8
photographic data 5, 11–13, 15
    collage/assemblage 74
    documenting events 14–15
    and doing nothing 60–1, 66
photographic project 73
Piagetian developmental approach 141
plastic reading method 57
playing
    away from adult-centric designs 135–8, 144
    with children 78, 90
    gendered 80–1
    with toys 128–31
Playing and Reality (Winnicott) 78
play in the bag 90–1
plurality, community interconnectedness 83
postdevelopmentalism 1–3
post-humanist approaches 42, 48, 50, 71, 90, 98
post-modern thinking 58
post-qualitative inquiry 12, 19, 65, 96
Powell, S. 153
programmazione (educational planning) 111–12

qualitative inquiry 57
queer archive 31–3
Queering observation 41–2
questioning children 76

reciprocal talk 77–8
recycling research 56–8, 67
Reggio Emilia Approach 8, 108–9, 111, 114, 117
relational communication 85–6
researching self 13, 19, 50. *See also* self data
response-ability 71–2
re-turning concept 55–7, 67–8
routine and everyday happenings 48–50
Roy, A. 89

Scarlet, R. R. 71
scientization of the child 24

Scollan, A. 8, 107–20
Scuole dell'infanzia 109, 111–12. *See also* Reggio Emilia Approach
self data 14
self images 18
Semenec, P. 7–8, 95–104
sensing of matter 6, 23
sequence organization 111
    interactions 111
situated knowledges 42
Skeggs, B. 44
sketchbook 9, 151–3
social class 43, 44
social stereotypes and injustices 85–6
sociomaterial theory 8
Somerville, M. 153
sound/earworms 7–8, 97–9, 103, 104 n.3. *See also* earworms
Springgay, S. 26, 32–4
STEM media 130–1
Stewart, K. 40, 41, 45–7
St. Pierre, E. A. 65
Supertoy project 78–83
Supertoys: A User's Manual 82
Supertoys Last All Summer Long (Aldiss) 78
Supertoys: Play, Affective Machines and Object Relations 79
sympoiesis 57, 67

talking methodologies 42
thinking 55–6, 58
tinkering, child-toy-text assemblages 127–30
    and assemblages 141–3
    attachment pattern 138–41
    child participants 132
    with developmentalist research and design 143–4
    Go-Pro cameras 133
    museum 132
    Nexus analysis 133–5
    playing away with adult-centric designs 135–8
    STEM media 130–1
    toys as co-actants 138–41
Totalitarianism 83

toys and materials 8–9
toys and play 78. *See also* gender-free toy design; Supertoy project
Toys: Are they Playing with You? 73
Toy Story 78–9
traditional observation 149–51
    ethnographic writing 151–2
transcorporeality 6–7, 41, 52
transformative education 73
troubling developmentalism 2
Truman, S. E. 26, 32–4
Tsing, A. L. 49, 51, 80
turn-taking conversation 111

verbal contributions 111
video-recorded interactions/observation 8, 95–8, 101–2

Viruru, R. 25
visual data generation 11–12, 19
visual optics/observation 4, 6, 59
void/emptiness. *See* nothingness

Walkerdine, V 24
Wallis, N. 27
Willink, K. 100
Winnicott's object relations theory 78–81, 92 n.1
without reading practice 6. *See also* observing-then-reading
Wohlwend, K. E. 8, 127–44
Wolff, K. 56
working-class women 42–4
worldhood 58–9
worlding(s) 47, 56, 58

www.ingramcontent.com/pod-product-compliance
Lightning Source LLC
Chambersburg PA
CBHW052125300426
44116CB00010B/1791